P9-DBQ-835

THE WORKING
ACTOR'S TOOLKIT

THE WORKING ACTOR'S TOOLKIT

Jean Schiffman

HEINEMANN
Portsmouth, NH

Heinemann
A division of Reed Elsevier Inc.
361 Hanover Street
Portsmouth, NH 03801-3912
www.heinemann.com

Offices and agents throughout the world

Copyright ©2003 by Jean Schiffman. All rights reserved. No part of this book may be reproduced in any form or by any electronic or mechanical means, including information storage and retrieval systems, without permission in writing from the publisher, except by a reviewer, who may quote brief passages in a review.

Editor: Lisa A. Barnett
Cover design: Catherine Hawkes/Cat & Mouse Design
Manufacturing: Louise Richardson

Printed in the United States of America on acid-free paper

06 05 04 03   VP   1 2 3 4 5

To my supportive husband, Stephen Kerr,
and to my mother, Muriel Schiffman,
always my biggest fan
in all my artistic endeavors.

CONTENTS

ACKNOWLEDGMENTS

Special thanks to Rob Kendt, editor of *Back Stage West,* where most of the material in this book first appeared; to my most influential acting teacher, Jean Shelton; and to all the actors, directors, playwrights, teachers, and other professionals who so generously share their expertise with me time and time again.

INTRODUCTION

This book is not a primer. It won't teach beginners the A-B-C's of acting. It won't lead you, step by step, through techniques. It does not purport to cover all bases.

Instead, this book has a more eccentric and idiosyncratic approach. It discusses craft-related issues that may concern—in some cases even preoccupy—the everyday working actor but that are often overlooked in the more traditional acting texts.

Its thirty-five chapters were chosen from among a hundred-plus articles I wrote for *Back Stage West,* Los Angeles' actors' trade weekly, over a period of about five years, in a biweekly column called "The Craft." In most of those columns, I interviewed several practitioners—actors, teachers, directors—and referred to the theories and techniques of various master teachers—Uta Hagen, Sanford Meisner, Constantin Stanislavski, and others—in order to present a balanced perspective on the topic at hand. I also occasionally fell back on my own admittedly limited experience, studying acting in the San Francisco Bay Area and working in a mid-sized, downtown San Francisco ensemble that I cofounded in the mid-1970s. The point I kept in mind, while writing those columns and preparing this book, is that there is no one way to act, and no one approach works for all actors.

In selecting columns for this book, I eliminated many on the basic skills—objectives, obstacles, actions, subtext, sense memory, given circumstances, physical work, voice work—on the assumption that you, a working actor, already know the building blocks for creating a performance. I also passed over specific methods taught by masters, from F. Mathias Alexander's physical training to Keith Johnstone's "impro" to Vsevolod Meyerhold's biomechanics; whole books have been dedicated to those approaches, and I could not do them justice here.

I looked instead for an eclectic range of subjects, from the seemingly trivial—what nonsmokers (or ex-smokers) can do if they have to light up in a play or film (Chapter 19)—to the profound—what is the secret of creating a deep relationship with your co-actor (Chapter 3)? I looked for concrete, practical advice (how to memorize, Chapter 27) as well as more esoteric discussions (how to cope with critical reviews, Chapter 34).

The chapters are grouped loosely into six sections, meant to open the floor for lively discourse on a broad range of topics. I purposely looked for a diversity of opinions, which means that in some chapters, my interviewees and cited sources may disagree with one another, and it's up to you to choose which theory you believe in, or which method works best for you. I sometimes jump into the fray and express my own opinion—but it's only one person's opinion, of course.

However, certain truths do emerge, elements of acting that I consider indisputable. Among them are the need to dig deep and personalize; to be specific; to avoid cliché; to take risks; to *behave* (play actions, pursue objectives) but not *indicate;* to find your place in the story that's being told; to remember that in the end, in most cases, less is more.

This book makes the assumption that you too will jump into the fray and formulate—or continue to develop—your own ideas. As Susan Sarandon said in an interview, "Acting is addictive; you can't get it right, and therefore you just keep trying."

Chapter 1

LISTEN UP!

The first and perhaps the hardest lesson I ever learned about acting was how to listen. I was working on a simple two-person scene—from *Liliom* by Ferenc Molnar, as I recall—but no matter what I did, my teacher, Jean Shelton, interrupted me. "Darling," she said. And said. And said again. "You're not *listening*." What on earth did she mean?

In Acting 1A in college, when the teacher told us to listen, we obediently hunched forward and cocked our ears and assumed intense facial expressions. We had the "attitude" of listening. We thought we were listening. But we weren't really listening.

Los Angeles acting teacher Judith Weston told me that some of her students think that as long as they hear their cues, they're listening.

I learned soon enough what listening is *not*: It is not "indicating" listening. It is not anticipating what you're going to hear. It is not hearing the words yet failing to deeply absorb them. It's something else entirely. I'm convinced you use a certain, minimal part of your brain when you focus intently on the other person's *words;* maybe you can even repeat them verbatim. But when you're concentrating in that single-minded, intent way, you've shut off the part of your brain that allows you to understand the language on a more impressionistic level. And you're too tense to notice the nuances, so the words fail to affect you on all levels: emotional, sensorial, and intellectual.

The kind of deep, relaxed listening that's required for acting means using your mind in a different way. And it involves taking the time to "process"—that is, to fully soak up what has just been said in order to respond in an organic way. But there's even more than that to what Uta Hagen calls *active listening.*

Here's a test for you, based on Hagen's comments in *A Challenge for the Actor.* Ask someone to tell you a rather complicated, detailed narrative, a paragraph or two in length. Did you see specific images in your mind as she told you the story? Can you paraphrase the story? If so, you're probably listening. (Weston notes in her book *Directing Actors* that if a film actor's lines are coming out exactly the same take after take, that actor is probably *not* listening.)

But there's listening and there's listening. On stage and on screen, we want to use more senses than just our sense of hearing.

What senses would those be? Weston writes that eye contact is a tool to enhance listening. That way, you are looking for deeper meaning, for physical clues—facial expressions, tics, unconscious gestures that reveal more than the words themselves. On the other hand, you don't want to go overboard with that technique: In real life we don't "eyeball" each other constantly. So you also need to listen to the vocal timbre, inflection, and volume of the other actor; you can even smell him, Weston suggests!

Of course, the point is that you must allow all this sensorial input to affect you. The other actor's words, grimaces, tone of voice, body language— all that must roil around inside you, meshing with your own personal gestalt and with your character's stuff.

Out of all that mishmash your lines emerge, hopefully intuitively and spontaneously, based on your identification with your character's circumstances, objectives, etc., and without such a delay that the director is yelling, "Pick up your cues!"

Are there dangers inherent in too much true listening? I believe not. In fact, I've seen good actors go astray by focusing too much on their own inner life and too little on listening. Many teachers have abandoned the Method's affective memory exercise (sensorially dredging up a specific personal experience to activate a needed feeling) because actors sometimes misuse it, tapping into personal emotions at the expense of connecting with onstage realities.

Weston has found in her classes that almost every acting problem can be solved by more active listening. She thinks it's the best tool an actor has, and that it prevents overacting. (Stanislavski approached the concept of listening from a broader perspective, calling it *communion,* by which he meant the listening-connection you establish with the audience, with yourself, *and* with the other actors.) Danny Glover, in an *Inside the Actors Studio* interview, said, "Listening is the key [to acting]. Listening and relaxing, because if you're not relaxed you can't listen." And as Joan Allen once pointed out in an interview in *Back Stage West,* if you lose your focus when acting, you can regain it by turning outward, by really listening.

What prevents actors from doing such a seemingly simple thing? Weston told me that one big culprit is the pre-set line reading (which you may not even know you're doing). To jog her students out of those patterns and cadences, she has them improvise the scene, paraphrase the lines, and gradually move to the lines as written. Or she has them go through the scene three times, each time playing a different action (for example, demand, beg, and seduce). Sometimes she has them read their lines very, very slowly, and/or very, very loudly, or even while hitting the couch with a pillow. She said, "This creates an energy strong enough to break through whatever energy they have invested in their preconceived line reading. Then they can be open to stimuli coming from the other actor."

Are there other ways to encourage the elusive art of listening?

Hagen advises that women work on the silent role in August Strindberg's two-character one-act, *The Stronger*. Great idea. Men might try Peter in Albee's *The Zoo Story*.

A helpful classroom exercise is for two actors to exchange the lines of their scene while moving farther and farther apart, until they're in different rooms shouting to be heard, and straining to listen and stay connected as though by an invisible cord. In that exercise, you have only your hearing to rely on, so you can see how deeply you need to use that particular sense.

Of course, the late Sandy Meisner's famous exercises, in which two actors repeatedly exchange the same two lines of dialogue, are very helpful at sensitizing you to meaning beyond words, to subtext.

Weston summed up for me her definition of listening: "It's really more like surrendering to your scene partner, giving your attention and concentration to your partner, letting your partner's feelings be more important than your feelings." She added, "We don't do it much in real life . . . that's why it has to be learned as an acting technique."

Chapter 2

THE CHARACTER AND "I"

I once interviewed Royal Shakespeare Company actress Monica Dolan, who I'd just seen in *The Taming of the Shew,* and she made a curious comment. "One of my directors taught me something very important," she said, "to always say 'she' when talking about the character. I find it useful. When you start doing what *you* would do in a situation rather than what your character would do, then you're not really being the character." When I told her I was taught just the opposite, she seemed surprised.

And *I* was surprised when it turned out the director she was referring to was none other than Mike Leigh. Because the actors in Mike Leigh's films always seem so natural and connected, it struck me as odd that he would advise them to separate from their characters—if only semantically. My teacher, Jean Shelton, always said, "At the end of the day, the words of the playwright and you—you in a funny hat and glasses, maybe—that's the character."

British actor, director, and teacher Adrian Brine points out in *A Shakespearean Actor Prepares,* "The character reveals itself in the way it reacts to the situation. Acting is chiefly a question of *re-*acting." The context of his comment is a discussion of how young actors sometimes get confused by Stanislavski's "magic if" exercises, wherein the actor asks, "What would I do if I were in my character's circumstances?" That question has been taken to mean that "the actor should somehow identify with the role," writes Brine, "whereas Stanislavski wrote about the 'circumstances,' the situation." Brine goes on to say, "The introduction of the concept 'I' often blocks an actor. 'I would never react like Lady Macbeth,' said a student once . . . The director said, 'But you might know someone who would. . . . Of course *you* are not like Lady Macbeth. But forget *you.*'"

Forget you?

Part of what Brine says makes sense to me: Acting, as he points out, isn't about playing a general, static idea of a character; it's about behaving in reaction to given circumstances and according to your objective, and we'll talk more about that below.

On the other hand, I think unless you can find a part of yourself that *is* like Lady Macbeth, you *will* be playing a general idea of her. Uta Hagen, who advocates the use of the personal pronoun when thinking about your character, suggests imagining that the character you are working on is *you*. For example, she says, in preparing to play Blanche in *A Streetcar Named Desire,* in your mind you'd think, *I* grew up in Belle Reve. Hagen realizes this trick won't necessarily make you believe you are the character, but it will lead you to find experiences in your own life that relate to your character's circumstances. What is *your* Belle Reve?

Similarly, Bobby Weinapple, a San Francisco actor/teacher/director, encourages his students to find a part of themselves that corresponds to the character and magnify it. "We tend to focus on how people are different," he said, "but at our core I think we're more similar than anything. . . . I've felt the impulse to kill. If I can accept that I can be pretty cruel sometimes, and I'm not afraid of that, then [for a role] I want to find that part of myself and 'visit' it. I know I'm doing it in the pretend world and I relish it." He added, "We've all wanted to be Iago at times."

Art Manke, a director/actor at Los Angeles' A Noise Within, is, like Hagen, "adamant" about always referring to characters in the first person. "I think it's especially helpful when working on the classics," he said. "If you're having trouble identifying with a king or queen or prince, it only helps the integration process if you think in the first person."

"I remember being corrected in acting classes [to say 'I']," said Los Angeles actor Patrick Kerr, a graduate of Yale Drama School. I asked him which he uses nowadays. Both, it seems, depending on the role: "Sometimes 'I' is more appropriate, sometimes 'he.'"

For example, his role as the Player King in *Hamlet* at California Shakespeare Festival was a definite 'I': "Why would I bother making a biography for an actor like the Player King when I *am* one and can use my own resources?"

On the other hand, he also played Grumio in *The Taming of the Shrew*—"not remotely me, definitely 'him.'" Once he'd acknowledged Grumio's circumstances and identified with them ("He works for this guy who's pretty touchy. I've never been a servant but I know what it means to struggle and try to do the best you can"), he found his way into the character physically: "I was standing and I realized I was holding my body stiffly, with my fingers splayed. And that became my hallmark for his character. The mind-set just followed from that."

For Kerr, as a general rule the most important thing is communicating truthfully with the other actors. The next most important thing is personalization. "Buzz [in *Love! Valour! Compassion!* at Berkeley Repertory Theatre] was another 'I.' He's a gay man without a boyfriend and so am I. He's a gay man who perceives himself as unattractive and a clown and I am all those things." The geek Noel that he played as a recurring role on *Frasier* is "definitely a 'him,'" but Kerr has found ways to identify with him. "I have the failsafe when I'm offstage—'Well, it wasn't me, it was the character'," he laughed. "But of course it's me—certain aspects of me. Acting is telling the truth." (And, as Spencer Tracy reputedly said, "Not bumping into the furniture.")

He advises focusing mainly on (and identifying with) what your character wants. "As actors we're always fighting—that's the nature of playing actions," he said. "Leave your feelings alone, play the actions. The gravy is the feelings. They'll be there if you're fighting for something you believe in."

Shelton, who emphasizes text analysis in her classes (see Chapter 26, "Script Analysis"), elaborated further: "You *never* think about what you would do *or* about what your character would do," she said firmly. "You think about what you're saying and what you want and why you want it and why you're here saying it. Otherwise you're playing for result. The dialogue will tell you where your character is coming from, why you're saying it. If you go beyond that, you're imitating life."

Should you think of your character as "me"? "Absolutely!" responded Shelton. "There's no one here but you! The character is the sum total of what you say, want, do. It's *you* doing all those things, maybe behaving in a way you've never behaved before." She added, "You have to have behavior, not just emotion."

"Mamet says the character does not pre-exist," pointed out Weinapple. "The character is the place where you and the text meet. I don't think there *is* a 'what the character would do.' The character is me and the text." He suggested a way of looking at it: "I think of something I know as an actor that the character doesn't know. For example, Amanda [in *The Glass Menagerie*] doesn't know she's controlling. But the actor playing Amanda needs to know. So in my work I'd try to find the place within myself that needs to control."

"Maybe if you have an actor who can't personalize, you tell her to use 'I,'" mused Los Angeles actor/teacher Wendy Phillips, who has starred in such primetime series as *Falcon Crest, Savannah, Promised Land,* and others, "and if you have an actor who's too subjective, you tell her to use 'she.'" Good point—different strokes, yadda yadda. Just so should an actor choose the pronoun that best enables him or her to connect, because ultimately that is your most sacred task as an actor. As E.M. Forster wrote, "Only connect."

Chapter 3

CHEMICAL REACTIONS

Chemistry: Tom Hanks and Meg Ryan have it. So did Bogie and Bacall. Redford and Newman. If critics fail to perceive a strong connection between two actors, they blame it on chemistry, as though through some quirk of genetic composition the two simply don't click on stage or screen. But it's not that scientific—or mystical. It's a matter of good acting—relating to your partner in the deepest possible way. And there are exercises you can do to help you get to that profound level.

Judith Weston, in a chapter called "Listening and Talking" in her book *Directing Actors,* writes, "When actors are said to have chemistry together, it means they listen to each other, they engage, they 'play off' each other. Romantic leads don't have to sleep together—they don't even have to like each other—as long as they listen. Cary Grant had chemistry with more leading ladies than probably any other actor in the history of movies—because he always listened, always put his full, relaxed concentration on his partner."

Listening goes a long way toward establishing a vibrant connection, but you'll need to go a little farther than that toward actually igniting the requisite flame if it's a sexual rapport that's required.

Los Angeles teacher/director Richard Seyd noted that it's hard for actors to create sexual chemical reactions unless they're comfortable with their own sexuality. "If both actors are comfortable, and they're unafraid to let their sexuality exist onstage, their lack of chemistry is because they have not developed a connection," he said. He pointed out that a connection of this type is subjective; it's hard for the actors themselves to see whether the so-called chemistry is there. Thus the director must look for it. "If you are inside the connection, you're not thinking about it, and if you're outside and thinking about it, then you probably don't have it," explained Richard.

He has a few exercises to help his students learn how to connect. "Actors and lovers are the only two people who make eye contact for extended periods of time," he said. So he has couples sit opposite each other, hold hands, and eyeball each other, with an egg timer or third person signaling the end of the exercise so that neither actor has to think about it. You can blink but you can't break eye contact or talk. "It's an old therapeutic exercise. It works," he said.

Or he suggests that the actors find a comfortable position where they can hold each other and synchronize their breathing: "Do anything you can do on a sensorial level to make that connection," he advised.

The rest, he said, has to do with fantasy—that is, fantasies about the person you're working with. "I always advise people to acknowledge at the beginning of the process that you're not going to have a [real-life] relationship," said Seyd. "Then you'll feel comfortable crossing the line. Otherwise one person is going, 'Oh my god, I'm getting incredible energy from this person. Is he attracted to me?' If you're working with someone you don't want a relationship with, [that concern] can make you pull back." He added, "There's nothing more pure than falling in love onstage because it's without repercussions."

Ivana Chubbuck, also a Los Angeles teacher, shared with me a method she developed to create instant chemistry, and these exercises go farther than Seyd's and are wonderfully specific. By way of introduction, she described the coaching she did on a film by her husband, Lyndon Chubbuck: *The War Bride*, a Canadian-English coproduction featuring Brenda Fricker.

Two of the film's main actors, Anna Friel and Aden Young, needed to experience intense mutual attraction, strong enough to compel them to marry despite the fact that their characters are of different nationalities. However, Friel and Young are two entirely different types of people with different life priorities, and they did not immediately connect.

Of course, the techniques normally used by actors to create sexual vibes were available to Friel and Young: 1) focus on at least one thing you really find appealing about the other person, and 2) if all else fails, use a substitution. However, the Chubbucks say that that's all well and good, but technique #1 is likely to create a superficial, banal response—Lyndon likened it to walking into a bar and being attracted to someone on a purely physical basis. "If you don't have the emotional depth," he said, "the sexual connection can be banal. We want to see people who are profoundly in love, not only wanting to get laid." And technique #2 is not visceral and immediate and spontaneous. Neither technique creates the depth of connection that Friel and Young needed, the kind of connection that exudes charm, power, and vulnerability.

So Ivana took each actor aside to find out what aspects of their personal history they shared. She was looking for something "very deep and dark, a primal trauma that happened to both of them." Not surprisingly, she found one. When you think about it, you probably share some painful experience with just about anyone you meet, from the bus driver to your acting teacher.

Lyndon elaborated: "You can find things you like about someone, you can turn yourself on to them, but you can go much farther; you can create a profound connection. Maybe your father is dying of cancer. Well, *my* father is dying of cancer."

"Or," said Ivana, "Jean's father has a disease, *your* father has cancer. See, Jean, he picked that up from you."

"Actually, it's my mother who has a disease, and a good friend who has cancer," I said. But the Chubbucks were right. Lyndon and I had established, briefly, a connection around pain, and if we were acting together, we'd develop that connection. With Ivana's help, Friel and Young found that connection and bonded over it.

The point is, when two people feel each other's pain (to use a cliché), they connect on a deep level. They care about each other because they identify with each other. "I am you and you are me . . ." And it goes without saying that actors know from pain. As Lyndon pointed out, people tend to become artists because they have a deep emotional reservoir, and because they want to make grace with their personal traumas.

So how do you go about finding out what the other person's secret nightmares and bad memories are, whether they be about an abusive childhood, a broken heart, a death, a life-threatening illness, an addiction? The best way is to get together with your costar for a chat and to confess to him or her your own painful experiences or issues. "You've got to prime the pump," advised Ivana. The more honest and open you are, the more likely your costar will respond in kind. Once you've found an incident or feeling in common, you're probably home free. The two of you will share a secret understanding, a vulnerability, that will seep into your stage or screen work.

If your costar is unwilling to go there, it's up to you. Ivana suggests first thinking about the "trauma or insecurity that most defines you," then looking deeply at the other person and seeing in his or her eyes "the pain, sadness, and rage that comes from having experienced the same thing."

Either way you approach it, this is an amazingly quick way of bonding. Ivana noted that Taylor Hackford, directing Keanu Reeves and Charlize Theron in *Devil's Advocate,* had them hang out together for three weeks wearing wedding rings to feel close. However, those three weeks didn't quite do the trick; Theron felt something was missing. At her request, Ivana was flown to New York to coach her. Ivana told Theron to ask Reeves specific personal questions. Within three hours, said Ivana, they'd united over shared pain. (Reeves didn't know at the time that Theron had been coached to do this.)

Of course there are different types of connections required depending upon the script's demands. Here's a tip on playing a parent. Ivana worked with Anna Friel in *The War Bride* to help her relate to a baby. Friel, 23 at the time, had never been a mother and was at a loss in creating a believable relationship with the babies who were playing her child. "As a parent you feel that a child represents a second chance to fix the stuff that happened to you when you were young," explained Ivana, who is herself a mother whose own mother constantly told her she was ugly and dumb. "A child is a little you." She coached Friel to imagine the baby as a little version of herself, to put her own issues into the baby's eyes. That naturally brought out in Friel the deepest possible sense of caring and protecting and closeness. The baby was an extension of herself. No "acting" was needed; the chemistry was there. Ivana suggests trying this out on friends' kids if you don't have kids yourself. Of course it also works if you're playing the parent of an adult child.

Most commonly, though, when we think of chemistry between actors, we think of sexuality. Ivana has a technique that can be used after you've created that emotional bond, to layer on the sexual element. Imagine your kinkiest fantasy and put your costar into that scenario in your mind. Naturally, your costar won't know what you're thinking, but Ivana guarantees a warm response. Be sure it's not a generic sexual fantasy—it must be personal to you, very private. She recommends this technique for auditions as well. You can use it on whomever you're reading with, along with the technique of seeing in their eyes a pain that corresponds to your own pain. You are thereby forging a quick-and-dirty but deep link. She also suggests trying it on casting directors, directors, or producers to create a special rapport that will subliminally enhance their perceptions of you. It shouldn't take more than 30 seconds to do all this, and you can do it while talking.

Lyndon vouches for these shortcuts to chemistry. Ivana was recently coaching a film star and suggested she try them out on everybody she encountered. Lyndon, who had known the actor for years, happened to walk into the room. In the course of what he described as a casual, ten-second chit-chat with her about dogs, he found himself thinking that she was much more attractive and interesting than he'd ever realized. She wasn't overtly sexual, or flattering, or anything like that—but he somehow became aware of her on a deeper level than previously. It was only afterward that his wife told him that the actor was doing the instant-chemistry exercise.

Chemistry is an essential ingredient in creating onscreen and onstage friendships, love relationships, and familial bonds. "It's an actor's duty to connect to whoever you're relating to," said Ivana. If it's true that there are no new plots under the sun, what we want to see onstage and onscreen is this particular, unpredictable, and utterly unique relationship.

Chapter 4

REAL-LIFE CHARACTERS

When blonde actor Lorri Holt entered as Hillary Clinton in Michelle Carter's witty stage play *Hillary and Soon-Yi Shop for Ties*, the audience burst out laughing. I think it was because Holt looked so amazingly like the former First Lady. As the play went on, it was clear that Holt not only resembled Hillary but had also created a multifaceted persona that enlarged our perception of that familiar media figure. Even if she hadn't been such a dead ringer for Rodham Clinton, it would still have been an enlightening performance.

How do actors approach the challenge of playing a real person, living or dead? Research, of course, is essential. In *Actors on Acting*, Rip Torn says that to play Walt Whitman, he read fifteen or twenty books, including seven biographies, plus all of Whitman's poetry, etc. Similarly, Lorri Holt read bits and pieces of lots of books about Hillary, and every article that came along, but found especially helpful a book of quotes uttered by Hillary herself.

On the other hand, Michael Gene Sullivan—who bears an uncanny resemblance to the late Huey P. Newton—found it more helpful to explore what *others* said about the chameleon-like Black Panther leader. After playing Newton in Robert Alexander's *A Servant of the People*, Michael went on to develop his own one-person play, *Did Anyone Ever Tell You You Look Like Huey P. Newton?* He read Newton's writings, watched videotapes of Newton's TV appearances. "When people are writing about themselves, it's always their best self," he noted. "With such a monumental figure, a large part of the truth is in how *others* interpreted him."

He also believes it's crucial to research the era and milieu in which the person lived. "If you're playing Abe Lincoln, read de Tocqueville," he advised. "Otherwise, you're just playing the person, not the world they inhabited. . . . I think some actors think the person they're playing is complete, that history began and ended with that character."

David Ramsey, who was preparing for the title role in the Fox biopic *Ali* when I phoned him in 1999, was very much aware that boxer Muhammad Ali, at the age he played him (eighteen to thirty-three), lived in a different world. Understanding the importance of extrapolating from his own personal experiences when working on any character, Ramsey wondered, "What do I take to compare to living in the '60s, saying to the press things like, 'No Viet Cong ever called me a nigger'? I'm going to have to pretend—that is, to act. I can relate to being a black man, but how he manipulated the media, his fire, his bravery, his position in religion, that I cannot relate to, me in my late twenties living in Los Angeles in 1999. But I can imagine it."

Whether playing real or fictional characters, you of course want to find as many ways to connect to them as you can. The difficulty with a real person, though, is that your research will reveal baffling contradictions. Still, you'll want to look for traits you can identify with, and emphasize them—providing those particular traits serve the script. Rip Torn, a lifelong hard worker, was able to identify with Whitman's work ethic. "I learned from the descriptions of his contemporaries the way he looked, the way he acted. And from all those qualities I chose the ones which would best represent him," Torn is quoted as saying. "I select my elements by the way I choose to walk, the way I move, the way my voice operates, the actual pitch of it . . . so while my identification is instinctive, my selectivity is conscious."

Which brings us to the physical. Holt found that she could initially ground herself by making deliberate physical choices and then going deeper in rehearsal. She worked on holding her mouth, her hands, her body like Hillary does. On the other hand, it's tricky: Holt observed that Hillary's voice had little variation in tone, which would be boring on stage. "I try to take some of what she does and adapt it," explained Holt.

Laurel Ollstein ran across a similar problem with the solo show she wrote, *Laughter, Hope and a Sock in the Eye*, about the witty writer Dorothy Parker. When she listened to a recording of Parker reading her work, she discovered that the writer had an affected accent, "more like Katharine Hepburn than what I expected of a hard-boiled writer." Ollstein figured that accent would shock audiences, so she combined the reality with her initial idea of what Parker sounded like.

Like Dorothy Parker, Ollstein is short and dark (although that's as far as the resemblance goes), which helped her create a sense of Parker as a short woman who led her life among tall men, their equal in every way but height, and she cut her hair in Parker's trademark bangs. Other than that, though, Ollstein focused mostly on Parker's inner workings, what made her do and say what she did. "Just doing an imitation of someone isn't really acting," she said. But she did point out that because Dorothy Parker was a writer, people are unfamiliar with what she sounded like, or with her mannerisms. That made it easier for Ollstein to come up with her own interpretation of the essence of the woman.

Sullivan had just the opposite problem: Everybody seems to have an opinion about what Huey Newton was like. Like Ollstein, though, Sullivan discovered that Newton's actual voice wouldn't really work on stage; it was irritatingly nasal. "I didn't try to copy his walk or speech," said Sullivan. "I wanted to get across his spirit, not just an impersonation." Because Newton was such an extreme and contradictory figure, Sullivan knew early on that his main goal would be to convey Newton's passion, torments, and frustrations, "his own inability to do all the things he wanted to do, as a human being set up as an icon." Added Sullivan, "If people come out of the show saying that I looked and sounded just like Huey, then I failed. But if they come out feeling enthusiastic about the political ideas he's bringing up, then I succeeded."

David Ramsey too was very conscious of the fact that Muhammad Ali is an icon, yet a complicated person who's perceived in many ways by many people. "You just try to be as honest as you can" in depicting him, he said. He trained in the ring for three hours a day to prep himself for the role, and at 210 pounds and 6'3" he looks not unlike the champion fighter at that age. He also worked on Ali's distinctive Louisville accent and when I talked to him was a little concerned about keeping track of the changes in Ali's vocal quality over the course of fifteen years (Ali's voice got lower and more controlled and his speech got slower), since the film was to be shot out of sequence. But his main goal was to reveal Ali's spirit. "I don't think there's any difference in playing fictional or real characters," he said. "You're still going to use the 'what if.'"

That may be true, but there are certainly different fears going into a project in which you're somehow beholden to society's images of a particular real person. Holt confessed to being worried about "getting it completely right," and doing something "grossly inappropriate," or playing a parody. She wanted to portray the complexity of the woman, not merely the media image. "We're all so many different people," she said. "I came up against limitations—not knowing what she'd do in a particular situation, so making a wild guess. . . . You feel you have to know everything about the person, make discoveries no one else has made, and that the more you accumulate, the closer you get to understanding this person. Then at some point you hit this wall and realize you can never truly become this person." Holt had been obsessed by Hillary, partly because the physical resemblance is indeed strong. (When she attended a fundraiser at which Rodham Clinton was to speak, she sensed a buzz in the room when she entered, and several people asked her if she was related to Hillary.) She'd cultivated a Hillary hair-do, kept a rehearsal journal called "Keeping Up With Hillary." "After you hit that wall," said Holt, "you have some sort of breakthrough and come to an understanding that allows you access in an imaginative way." For her, that breakthrough came two weeks before opening, in the form of a dream in which she had to imperson-ate Hillary for real. "I think after that I relaxed a little more," she said. "I real-ized I can never actually be her, so I'll just do my best."

Similarly, Sullivan found himself absorbing a little too much of New-ton's personality when he appeared in *A Servant of the People*. "I had to come to grips with this tragically flawed hero of mine, and seeing similarities between myself and him," he told me. At one point he ranted at two co-actors whom he thought were not taking the show seriously enough. "Then I real-ized I was doing what Huey did—acting as if I know it all. Huey ended up very paranoid, thinking everyone was counterrevolutionary. And I started feeling that way."

Rip Torn, in *Actors on Acting*, says, "I never believe that I *am* the char-acter. I might believe it for a moment in the scene because I'm concentrating as the character would be, but that's about it." When helpful hotel clerks addressed him as "Mr. Whitman," he'd say, "He ain't here."

The most important advice for actors, said Michael Sullivan, is to real-ize that there is no single truth about a person. "You have to decide what aspects of that person best serve the play," he said. We talked about how Anthony Hopkins played Richard Nixon, in the 1995 film *Nixon*, as a desper-ate person who needed love, which didn't exactly make him sympathetic, but somehow made him human and understandable. I think if you can accom-plish that with your character, you've done a lot.

Chapter 5

STAGE VIOLENCE

Whether it be in the form of slaps, fisticuffs, or sword fights, stage violence presents two major problems: how to stay safe and how to be believable.

Slaps are the most common form of physical aggression most actors are likely to encounter. My friend, acting teacher Ed Hooks, once sent me a worried e-mail on the topic: "I've heard all sorts of conflicting advice on [slaps]," he wrote. "I'm always concerned that actors might hurt one another because there is an adrenaline rush when they are on stage." He continued, "Face-slapping is a continual conundrum. Everybody has a different idea about how to do it. Some people (me) suggest that the slapper make contact with the slappee on the neck area, just below the jaw. And the slappee really controls the apparent blow by the way she recoils. It needs to be choreographed, with the actors starting slowly and picking up speed as they work it out. But others emphatically say that actors should not make contact at all. Just do an air slap that comes close. Others suggest elaborate two-handed deals where the slapper makes contact with the palm of his own hand, or with the hand of the slappee." He added, "One night, I tried to demonstrate a slap in front of the class, and the actress I slapped didn't recoil. It stung her. So here I was *hitting* my student!! Good God! . . . it spooked me."

So: to slap or not to actually slap? And, whichever you choose, how do you do it most effectively?

"I feel there has to be some contact made or it doesn't work," actor/physical comedian Joan Mankin said. "Some people get very nervous about being touched violently and they want it to be as far as possible from the reality. Others really need the impact. People have very different pain thresholds."

"What about you?" I asked.

"I have a high threshold," said Mankin. "I welcome the impulse. It makes me respond. That doesn't mean I want to get hurt. . . . It's a very personal thing between the slapper and the slappee. . . . It's just like a kiss—it's a very intimate stage interaction that has to be approached with care and respect on both sides." Mankin, who practices every night before the show, recommended a cheek or temple smackeroo.

Whether choosing a fake or a real swat, choreography is essential. Uta Hagen warns that audiences are likely to start worrying about the actors rather than the characters if a fight is too convincing.

A college drama professor detailed for me his techniques for directing the real slap: "I start light to see how much the actor can take without hurting. Then I have the slapper back off from that, as during a performance the adrenaline will increase the power. . . . Slow mo, strong emotions and reactions are the keys for me. Avoid the ears (implosion), the eyes (ditto), and the jaw (the teeth). Hit the side of the neck for serious enemies or lovers and the side of the forehead for underlings and children. The shoulder even works as the slappee can raise it to protect himself."

Director Simon Levy pulled no punches in voting for the real thing. "*Wham!* Let 'em have it!" he e-mailed. "You can't fake a slap. Given that I've done most of my directing in intimate theatres . . . I discovered early on you have to haul off and do it. But *carefully*. Never hit the ear. *Never!* And keep that splayed finger away from the eye. You want to catch the person on the jawbone with a cupped hand. The jawbone's strong, the cupped hand softens the blow and makes a great sound. And if the actor getting slapped goes with the slap, it looks great and also softens the hit. It looks and sounds real because it *is*. A fake slap looks like what it is: fake. The whole purpose of a slap is that it's an expression of an emotionally intense moment." Note that Levy recommends the jawbone, whereas some others advise against it.

But Levy added that he always uses a fight choreographer. "I've arrogantly 'fight-directed' scenes I never should have and actors got hurt. [Now], whether it's a simple slap or a knock-down, drag-out free-for-all, I leave it to [a fight director] to physically tell the emotional story I want to tell. And he does, and nobody gets hurt." Indeed, smart actors ask at the audition if there will be a fight choreographer on the show; if not, they reconsider whether they want to participate. Certification by the Society of American Fight Directors is not essential, but adequate training (by established teachers) and experience are.

As for faking: the slappee can stand sideways and raise her upstage hand to her face in advance; then the slapper can whack that hand. Or, similarly masked from view, the slapper can grab the slappee's face with one hand and whack with the other—but actually hit his own hand.

And in those cases, a "knap" (the accompanying sound effect) is usually provided. If the slappee has her back to the audience, she can hold her hands low and clap them together where the audience can't see. Or the slapper, or both slapper and slappee, can provide the knap. Or other people, on or off-stage, can do so, but that's often hard to coordinate with the exact time the slap hits. The knap can also be on a soundtrack.

How you choose to present a slap depends on the size of the house, according to Bob Borwick, formerly with San Francisco's Academy of the Sword. "What type of space it is, proscenium, round, or three-quarters thrust, how close is the audience? . . . A proscenium is easiest for selling a [fake] slap because the audience is in one place right in front of you. Otherwise it gets tricky. But if you're a proficient actor/combatant with proper training, you'll find ways to surprise or distract the audience from the actual technique."

Maybe so, but how many of us are, especially women? Still, Borwick favors virtual slaps, particularly in larger houses. "If you really slap some-body, you don't get much of a sound, for one thing," he said. "Secondly, with a large house, a lot of stage combat techniques are designed to help the char-acter express himself physically. If you do a real slap, your aim has to be pin-point perfect, just below the cheekbone, avoiding eyes, ears, throat. You get popped in the ear once, and you'll hear that ringing maybe for days. Also, oftentimes the audience will be looking at the red mark on the slappee's cheek and wonder if they're really hurt rather than thinking about the drama in the scene."

He continued, "With a fake slap, we'll block them so that the slap is masked. We create distance between the two people, and no contact is made, but there's certainly a partnership between the two fighters. That allows the actors to express themselves fully, knowing the safety features involved. In a real slap, you have to control your body, and that quiets the body down and you won't be as aggressive physically as you want to be. I think a number of actors want a real slap; they feel like it helps them, and they think an audience won't buy a fake slap. . . . But if you practice it enough, you can sell it to an audience *and* keep yourself and your partner safe."

His colleague, Academy executive director Richard Lane, agreed. "The risk [involved in a real swipe] is too great," argued Lane. "No matter how nonviolent you are, your body sends autonomic messages when you take the shape of 'I'm going to throw a punch.' Your adrenal gland infuses your system with adrenaline, which doctors recognize as one of the most powerful drugs on the planet." He noted that J.D. Martinez, in his 1982 book *Combat Mime: A Non-Violent Approach to Stage Violence,* shows how an actual hit runs the potential of pinching a nerve at the point of contact on the face, or damaging a gland that lies just beneath the surface of the skin. "The Society of American Fight Directors has been looking at this issue for thirty years now, since our inception," pointed out Lane. "You injure a nerve, and you develop a perma-nent twitch. It's no accident that if you say our acronym, SAFD, quickly, it sounds like safety!" He added, "Theatre is the art of pretend, so why is it that violence has to be real? Nothing else onstage is as it is in real life."

A friend of mine who broke her nose in five places when a fake slap accidentally turned into a contact doozie might say, "Touché!" "I don't think being slapped for real has any place in theatre," she told me. She said that her slapper was so full of adrenaline he never realized he'd made contact (despite a crack so loud the audience gasped) until he saw blood everywhere. But she conceded that a real whack inevitably evokes a genuine emotional response.

It's that emotional response that is the prime concern of Jeffrey Bihr, an actor/director who has also taught stage combat. He said, "I've done both. There's nothing more fake than fake violence. It's right up there with fake romance and fake sexuality. It's ludicrous. It does the exact opposite of what it's supposed to do if it's badly done. If it's well done, it's an illusion. Even a real slap on some level is an illusion—the audience knows it's planned. So the question becomes, how well is the illusion staged, and what happens *after* the illusion? That's what'll make the moment work or not. When stage slaps are done with a knap and really well done and come suddenly, they can still be quite effective. But nothing seems more effective than to really slap."

What is Bihr's opinion of the correct position for the genuine article? Like most of the others I talked to, he cautioned against the eyes and jawline. "Hit with the flat of hand under the cheekbone," he advised. "The slapper should pull back to make a good slap sound. The force behind the slap should sound like it's great but not be great. The audience should gasp.

"More importantly," he went on, "it should bring up something in the actor, and that's what's often missing. What needs to happen is the slapper's reaction: I hit him in the face, how did he take it, is he going to hit me back, am I going to hit him again, how did that simple transaction change the nature of our relationship? *That's* where the slap lives. If that slap does not come out of a sudden urge for violence, then it doesn't look real no matter how it's staged. So the technique of the slap can be done in many different ways and must be professionally handled and clear, but really the most important parts—the set-up and what happens after—are more important than the slap itself."

Bihr added, "I would have this exact same conversation with you if we were talking about kissing." He agreed with the others that most directors are not capable of guiding an actor through this, or feel they aren't. He himself always calls in a fight director.

If you can get by without a fight director when staging a slap, you certainly need one when choreographing fisticuffs. Robert Goodwin of the Action Actors Academy in Los Angeles, who has been choreographing fight scenes for theatre and film for decades, concurred with this approach, saying firmly, "Safety first." He likes four hours of rehearsal for every twenty seconds of fisticuffs. Gregory Hoffman, resident fight director at San Francisco's American Conservatory Theater, suggests ten hours of rehearsal per one-minute fight scene in an ideal world but settles for half that . . . if he's lucky. (A minute is a very long fight; a short fight is two or three seconds.) Fight directors I talked to bemoaned inadequate time allotted for fight rehearsals, and being called in appallingly late in the game.

When slugging, actors cue each other, usually through eye contact, before striking a blow. Then the aggressor winds up to indicate he's going to attack and follows through with the "technique," which may be "misdirected" to avoid physical contact but otherwise is a "pulled move," stopping short at a safe point and going backwards from there. The victim's reaction follows, then his action. Scenes are rehearsed starting with super slo-mo and working up to 75 percent of normal speed (for the sake of maintaining control and so the audience can see what's going on).

Goodwin checks continually with the actors to make sure the moves work for them. "If they have a natural contrary reaction to what I'm asking them to do, I will change it," he said. "I don't want them to have to think about it." Actors, who are not usually born street fighters, are already bucking their natural instincts as well as dealing with basic acting concerns. If you're thinking too much about how to finesse a move that goes entirely against the grain, timing can break down, the cuing system can collapse, things can go seriously wrong.

The secret, all agreed, is "keep it simple, stupid."

"Stage combat, fight . . . these are the wrong words," exclaimed Lane, who prefers "illusion of conflict"—that is, "two actors manipulating an audience's imagination."

When Lane first started out, a director told him to "improvise a fight." Lane, who had never been in a fight in his life, immediately punched the other actor in the mouth. "I didn't know I was supposed to throw a punch at a target two inches away from the 'real' target," he said. Now he fixes the image of his partner in his mind, and when his opponent ducks, he still sees the image of his face floating in space, and that's what he attacks.

Good fight directors know that each actor's psychology and confidence level is different. Early on in Lane's career, he choreographed *Romeo and Juliet*. The actor playing Benvolio was intimidated by the sword fight and walked out of rehearsal in tears. Lane sat down and talked to Tybalt and Benvolio, discussing the scene, generating trust between them. Problem solved.

In another instance, Lane was showing a class how to pull hair. The aggressor extends his arm and holds onto the victim's hair; she grasps his wrist and pulls it *toward* her own head. The student he was using for the demonstration broke down in tears; she'd been in an abusive relationship and the action kindled emotional recall. "It's a dicey business," said Lane. "Some people get aggressive, some get scared, some carry a lot of baggage."

An actor may also have physical limitations. Hoffman had to make changes, when choreographing a show, for the sake of an actor who had recently hurt her back; he didn't want her to take risks in performance.

Of course, each *character's* psychology is different too, based on the demands of the text, so while the actor is dealing with her own personal demons regarding violence, she and the fight director will also be considering what kind of physical aggression is appropriate for her character as well. Slapping, punching, kicking, hair-pulling, choking?

Are the rules (and precautions) different for women when it comes to violence? The men I talked to insisted it's basically the same no matter who engages in the combat. But Erin Merritt, director of Woman's Will, an all-female Shakespeare company, conceded that whereas boys generally tend to tussle with their buddies, maybe take wrestling in school, girls are more likely to have studied dancing. "Women have an easier time learning the choreography but have fears of physical aggressiveness," she said. Stage combat, she noted, is about moving into another's space. "Some have been taught that girls should take up less space in the world. They have to remember to forget that." Goodwin, though, has found that once women let go they can actually be more aggressive than men and overpower them.

The set itself may present obstacles. Merritt choreographed differently for both stone and grass for an outdoor production of *Coriolanus,* to assure the safety of her cast. Hoffman pointed out another hazard of outdoor performances: Foggy nights can create moisture onstage.

As Bihr said in regard to slapping, here too the realism has to come from the actor's intent, not necessarily from the combat itself. Yet that's a Catch-22. The trick, pointed out Goodwin, is to sustain genuine, organic anger but not let it carry you away. "The victim is the one in control," he said. "The attacker has to follow the victim." You also have to not anticipate the punch, and your position in relation to the audience can help mask a tendency to do so (see Chapter 7, "Eeeek! Playing Fear," for a tip on avoiding anticipation).

"What takes actors out of character is fear," said Lane. "How can you act naturally as Willy Loman if you're afraid you're going to dislocate your son's jaw?" The solution, of course, is adequate training and rehearsal. Once that's accomplished, said Merritt, you'll have body memory, emotion, and backstory in place, and adrenaline will take care of the rest.

Yes, things can go wrong. Hoffman enumerated a few: You're too close to each other (as was the case, cited earlier, of my friend with the broken nose); you failed to make eye contact; someone was in the wrong place; a piece of furniture was inadvertently left onstage. The important thing, he said, is to acknowledge your fears and be honest about your abilities. En garde!

Chapter 6

THREE SHEETS
TO THE WIND:
PLAYING DRUNK

I t's a time-honored tradition for playwrights to create drunken characters. On the simplest level, staggering, red-nosed boozers can be amusing, as Dudley Moore proved. More importantly, as Chicago actor/teacher Ed Hooks observed, playwrights use alcohol to loosen the tongues of their characters and give them courage, thereby allowing for outrageously theatrical behavior and the revealing of truths. He noted Edward Albee's George and Martha, just for starters; *Who's Afraid of Virginia Woolf?* wouldn't exist if the characters weren't getting blitzed. Same with Eugene O'Neill's *Long Day's Journey into Night*, in which the effects of both drink and drugs catalyze the play's action and allow the characters to express their deepest feelings. Then there's Michael Cristofer's *The Shadow Box*, in which the wife, fortified by drink, confronts her husband's gay lover. Crocked characters are a fact of dramatic literature.

To play them, of course you don't have to prep by bellying up to the nearest bar, any more than you have to kill someone to play a murderer. Using as your resources your sense memory and observational skills, and a few physiological facts, you have all you need to play an inebriated character.

Playing drunk isn't easy, mind you. It's all too easy to play a crocked cliché. How do you avoid caricature and stereotype and make *your* boozer believable, whether the playwright's intention was for revelation or merely for chuckles?

Lesson #1: As with any aspect of acting, *be specific*. Hagen suggests focusing on the most "suggestible" area or areas of your body, then creating and abandoning yourself to a localized feeling of vulnerability. She allowed herself, for instance, to give in to weak, wobbly knees. She also focused on imagining her tongue feeling fat and swollen. Go back to your sense memory exercises for guidance.

Lesson #2: Once you've localized the physical manifestations of drunkenness, *work against them.* (This lesson applies to many other aspects of acting as well, for example, crying, or playing someone with a physical handicap, such as Laura in *The Glass Menagerie.* It also applies to any other substance, such as drugs: Let it affect your body, then act against it.) Hagen concentrated on bracing and strengthening those weak knees, on overarticulating around the thick tongue. These physical problems you've created for yourself are your obstacles; your task is to overcome them. Bay Area teacher Phil Bennett suggested finding a physical center of balance, and then, the more drunk you get, the more you try to re-establish that balance.

In *Acting Power,* Robert Cohen writes, "Play a drunkard by trying to walk a straight line with absolute precision." Your obstacle is whatever specific physical weaknesses are conspiring to prevent you from doing so.

"The drunkard," continues Cohen, "is not identifiable because he cannot walk a straight line but because he tries so hard to suppress his fear of being unable to do so." To play drunk, try very hard to act sober, because, as Hooks cautioned, you don't want to play the *result:* That way lies the dread cliché.

Lesson #3: *Research* the condition. Alcohol is a depressant (which is to say it doesn't necessarily make us frenzied); it loosens our inhibitions, both physical and emotional; it relaxes our muscles so we may feel like rag dolls; it intensifies our emotions, often making us sentimental and weepy; it may scramble our logical thinking processes. These facts are useful for choosing your physical sensations (see Lesson #1).

Among the common effects of inebriation: dizziness (you can create an instant sense memory, if you don't already have one, by simply spinning around) and lack of eye and manual focus. I myself, I regret to admit, have actually seen double, which involved a lot of intense squinting to try to refocus the images. San Francisco teacher Rachael Adler noted that when you're three sheets to the wind, your relationship to gravity changes, so your rhythm and movement change.

Lesson #4: *Observe* the condition (in others, naturally). Bennett recommends that his students watch the great comic actors as well: Dick Van Dyke, Buster Keaton, Charlie Chaplin, or the perpetually plowed Sebastian (Anthony Andrews) in the PBS series *Brideshead Revisited.*

Lesson #5: *Don't overdo it.* As Robert Cohen writes, "You need not protest too much; simply 'enough' will do." Hooks warned, "If you get too drunk onstage, you're going to lose the audience. They'll be thinking, Boy, that person sure is drunk—and that's *all* they'll be thinking." The more subtle the better, advised my own acting mentor, Jean Shelton.

Adler pointed out that your starting point in playing drunk may vary depending upon your own sensibilities. "A physically uptight actor with a rich emotional life might approach it differently than a repressed person who moves fluidly," she said. "Some need to initially approach it physically, others psychologically, others emotionally." But in the end your entire instrument should be affected.

Finally, don't forget that usually the scene is *not* about drunkenness per se; drunkenness is an element of the scene, a condition. Therefore, once you've conjured up the appropriate physical sensations, you might want to make some specific choices about when to struggle with that condition—a slur here and a slur there, suggested Shelton, so that you don't concentrate on being drunk to the detriment of playing your objective and everything else you need to do to make the scene work.

Above all, said Adler, don't hurt yourself, check out any rude impulses in advance with your co-actors—and have fun.

Cheers!

Chapter 7

EEEEK! PLAYING FEAR

How often have you seen otherwise perfectly good actors indicate fear and horror by bugging out their eyes? I can't really blame them. Playing panic convincingly was always one of my Achilles' heels too. I remember in one screwball comedy, no matter how much I tried to imagine that I was really being kidnapped, my expressions of alarm felt either phony or generic.

As Los Angeles acting teacher Ivana Chubbuck pointed out to me, audiences love to see the real McCoy, people practically peeing in their pants; why else are such reality shows as *Survivor* so popular? "Those people [on *Survivor*] don't know how to *not* show fear," she said. Actors need techniques to access terror that is just as palpable and personal, techniques that will work for stage, screen, and blue screen.

"Directors will say again and again that true organic fear is the hardest thing for actors to get to," continued Chubbuck. "All the telltale physical responses are involuntary—pupils contract, heartbeat quickens, adrenaline pumps into your system, skin blanches."

Don't lose heart, though. There *are* ways of reacting honestly and fearfully to imaginary situations, thus generating those involuntary reactions.

For actors there are two kinds of fear: quick-reaction (Run for your life! Here comes a dinosaur!), and sustained (you're playing the wife in *Dial M for Murder*). They require different approaches.

Uta Hagen, in *A Challenge for the Actor,* makes it sound easy. She has a rodent phobia, so she simply imagines a mouse or a rat and feels overwhelmed by revulsion. She says that imagining your most personally horrifying spectacle, whatever it may be, works for everyone. A doctor told her that such phobias are natural, a compressed symbol for the everyday and lifelong fears that we repress or don't understand. George Orwell knew all about it; remember the dreaded Room 101 in *1984*?

Chubbuck embroidered upon Hagen's suggestion: Don't just imagine rats; imagine you're in a small room and they're scampering all over you, burrowing in your orifices, biting your . . . well, you get the picture.

Still, even those images might not work for everyone. Los Angeles actor and teacher Wendy Phillips told me she has no really powerful phobias. The key for her is physical relaxation—getting as far away as she can mentally and physically from the scary event-to-be—followed by total commitment. "You can't psychologically sneak up on it," she said.

In a scene in the film *Bugsy*, Phillips had to slap Warren Beatty. She said they must have done the take fifty times. Each time, Beatty came to the scene with complete relaxation, no anticipation. "Every take, that slap worked for him emotionally," said Phillips. "I don't know how he did it. I don't know if I could do it. . . . The more relaxed and innocent you can get yourself, the better chance you have of reacting involuntarily."

As a regular on the TV show *Falcon Crest*, Phillips once had a scene in which her husband shoots himself in the head. By the time they got around to her close-up, the husband had been dismissed for the day. And a sound ordinance forbade any loud noises. "All I had to react to was the director whispering, 'And now—bang,'" she said. "I was like, this is *it*? A whispered bang? Usually I find on films if you ask for a sound cue, a bang, off-camera, that really helps."

"But what if it's a visual cue you're responding to?" I asked.

"It doesn't matter," said Phillips. "If you can get someone to bang a prop, your body will involuntarily react to that sound, and you make the adjustment that it's fear."

To keep the creeps going over a period of time, Phillips finds it helpful to create a silent verbal chant, along the lines of "Oh my God, please, please," and gives herself permission to work up to a frenzy in rehearsal. She relies upon that internal chant instead of on the other actor, then cuts back as needed in performance. I've tried that too, but it tended to feel hollow for me.

"Just know what you're afraid of, and jump in; don't work on the specificity," advised Phillips. "Just trust that it's there."

What we're talking about here, of course, is making the fear real for you personally. There is no type of fear, whether instant or sustained, that exists when you're acting other than your personal fear, your demons.

Chubbuck has a special technique for quickly contacting your deepest angst and maintaining it throughout a take or a scene. She connects the concept of *fear* to *action*. Our body and brain unconsciously create a fight or flight response, she told me, in order to overcome what's threatening us. So it's not just a matter of imagining something scary; it's a matter of activating that response. "It's the need to survive that actually creates fear, not the fearful situation itself," she said.

She led me through this simple exercise:

1. First, make a list of your fifteen to twenty strongest reasons for staying alive today, the things you most desperately need to do—you personally, of course, not your character. (I could dredge up only four.) Don't get lazy, said Chubbuck—investigate everything.

2. Then read the list aloud and choose the most obviously powerful one. "The best ones are always the ones you're in denial about," she said. If you're a parent, your choice will probably have to do with your child. I'm not. I chose a current important task: to help my aged father, the sole caregiver for my mother, who has Alzheimer's.

3. Chubbuck told me to imagine Dad smiling at me lovingly, gratefully. Then she told me to imagine myself *not there,* Dad all alone in the world, so desperate he's ready to take his own life.

4. Then I was to say to myself, over and over, "I've got to survive to keep this from happening," like a mantra. The final step is to let it go and trust it will work.

"When you see your worst nightmare come true," said Chubbuck, "then you go into survival mode, your heart rate will increase, stuff will happen to you." That "stuff" will manifest itself in your acting choices. You will be alive in the moment, reacting spontaneously and profoundly.

I confess my heart wasn't pounding, although I did have tears in my eyes. It probably didn't help that I was sitting at my computer in my sweats with a headset on. Chubbuck swears it works on all her students.

The exercise (once you've chosen your worst-case scenario, which you should do that morning) takes no more than twenty to thirty seconds; do it just before the camera rolls—"When you've got your five-minute warning, and they're tweaking the lights," Chubbuck said—or during rehearsal. I imagine in a play you could do it just after the stage manager calls places—unless, of course, the frightening thing happens after you've been onstage for a while, in which case we're back to the sudden, unanticipated attack of the maggots.

"Every thought, sound, sight forms a crevice in the brain," explained Chubbuck. "There isn't anything that happens to you that doesn't become memorized. So you can get to [those memories] quickly if you prepare. Trust that your body will go back to those places. If you think about it too much, you mindfuck yourself."

She emphasized that this fear-inducing trick is not meant to be a lengthy affective memory exercise; rather, it's short and immediate. "Don't pump yourself for two hours, there's nothing worse than that," she said. "It leaves you and others uncomfortable. . . . Thinking of your scariest moment—that just makes you vomit up old experiences, attempting to feel them again but never really feeling them that strongly. When you're on camera, the audience knows if you're lying or if you're vomiting up dead dog stories." (Gulp. I have been guilty of using the dead dog ploy. I thought it worked rather well at the time.)

She also noted that each time you tackle a new project, you'll need to reinvestigate what scenario works best for you at the moment. Just remember: The important thing is to imagine your most primal need today, then imagine what would happen if you weren't there to fulfill that need, then let your natural instincts propel you forward. The need to overcome, to survive, for a very tangible reason, is what will make the fear real. Said Chubbuck, "Fear is a good thing. It helps us take action."

To paraphrase Theodore Roosevelt, the only thing *not* to fear is fear itself.

Chapter 8

PLAYING PAIN AND DYING

In the 1999 Pulitzer Prize–winning drama *Wit*, set in a hospital, the central character, Dr. Vivian Bearing, introduces herself to the audience right at the top of the play, concluding her monologue with the words, *I've got less than two hours. Then: curtain.* She means that quite literally; before the play is over and the curtain descends, she will die of stage four ovarian cancer. And before she dies, she will suffer excruciating pain; she will say, *I have a fever of 101 spiking to 104. And I have bone metastases in my pelvis and both femurs. . . . I did not know there could be such pain on this earth.*

How does an actor experience pain and death onstage? And how does working on such a role affect you personally? I called Judith Light, the Emmy Award–winning actress (*One Life to Live*) who took over the role of Vivian from Kathleen Chalfant at Off-Broadway's Union Square Theater and went on the road with it. We talked prior to the play's opening in San Francisco, the last stop on the three-month, five-city tour.

This was Light's first venture back on stage after a lengthy TV career; she'd debuted on Broadway in *A Doll's House* with Liv Ullman in the early '70s. I asked her what initial research she did to prepare for the role.

"I read a lot of different books about death and dying," she said. Among them were Ernest Becker's *Denial of Death* and Victor Frankl's *Man's Search for Meaning.* (Still doing her homework, she jotted down the name of a book I mentioned, Sherwin B. Nuland's *How We Die.*) Also, one of her closest friends is an ovarian cancer survivor and shared her journal with Light.

But reading wasn't enough. At Cedars-Sinai Hospital Light talked to a doctor in gynecology-oncology and observed patients with ovarian cancer. "Both my maternal and paternal grandmothers died of cancer," she added. And other close friends, too, have died recently.

She was quick to note, though, that the idea isn't to bring all this

29

medical research on stage. If you do, you run the risk of overanalyzing and overintellectualizing the role. "I take it and then I throw it away," she said. The only thing that really counts is the moment onstage, when you're connecting with your fellow actors. "Do all the research, then focus on the circumstances," she cautioned. "What matters is what you're giving to the person you're in the scene with and what you're giving to audience."

Nevertheless, it's important to research the specifics. Light needed to understand just how ovarian cancer and chemotherapy affect the body of a fifty-year-old woman. She needed to know exactly where the pain would materialize, and how severe it would be. The illness and the pain influence the way you walk and stand, she pointed out. That's not to mention possible nausea, and ongoing discomfort in various parts of the body, and the effects of the various medications the character is taking.

Light relied to a great extent upon playwright Margaret Edson's words, rereading the text often. "When I say the line, *I want to tell you how it feels . . . the time for extreme measures has come, I am in terrible pain*—I have spent hours on those words, experiencing what those words mean," she said. "So subsequently it comes into my body. It's the homework that's taken me to that place. Substituting [the memory of] the day my dog died doesn't help me. I have had to do hours of work on the experience of those words."

The dead-doggie thing has always worked really well for me in conjuring up a certain type of aching sadness (and see more about the overused dead-pet trick in Chapter 7, "Eeeek! Playing Fear"), but I can see where it wouldn't apply here. In playing someone like Vivian Bearing, who's tough with a hidden core of vulnerability, and of course suffering physically as well as emotionally, you want to be struggling against the pain, not showing the audience how much it hurts (as we know, that rule holds true in just about any role for just about any physical or emotional condition—see Chapter 6, "Three Sheets to the Wind: Playing Drunk"). But first you do have to feel the pain, at least to some extent. And many of us need more than just a deep understanding of the words in order to create "terrible pain"—or, for that matter, any physical sensation. How to approach the task?

Through sense memory, natch. The reliably down-to-earth Uta Hagen in *A Challenge for the Actor* explains that once you determine exactly how the condition affects you, the next step is to find a "physical adjustment" to alleviate it. She warns that you can spend a lot of time trying to feel, say, extreme heat—but once you've imagined, for example, your shirt sticking to your skin, then you need to proceed to step two: perhaps pulling your shirt from your chest to feel the cool breeze. That action is your physical adjustment. It not only aids you in actually feeling the sensation you're striving for, it also keeps your behavior natural; you're *doing* something specific, as opposed to merely *showing* the audience how darned hot you are.

Does that second step apply when you're acting a condition as intense and unrelenting as pain from cancer? After all, there is no simple, concrete way to alleviate such pain. Or is there? I once had a sudden toothache so intense that I had to get up and run around the room until the pain medication kicked in. And I've seen videotapes of people with excruciating migraine headaches banging their head against the wall to counterattack the agony. Ouch. So maybe for even the deadliest pain there is a sort of involuntary physical adjustment, no matter how ineffectual it may be in reality. In any case, I would say do the homework required to locate your life-threatening pain specifically. I asked Judith Light, "If someone stopped you at any point in the play and asked you, 'Where does it hurt right now?' would you be able to answer?" She said yes, and after seeing her work in *Wit,* I believe her. "I find the place in myself where it's true that I hurt," she explained.

What are the traps in playing a dying person? "Avoiding melodrama would be the biggest thing," Light said. "Indicating pain, feeling sorry for yourself." Instead, she counseled, "Stay in the moment. Stay connected to the person you're playing the scene with. Be willing to be vulnerable." She added, "I have an unusual relationship with my manager, and he helps me stay centered. Have a person whose input you trust."

What about the psychological effect of living day to day—or for the length of a film shoot—with some who is sick and dying? Is it scary or depressing? Not for Light, who has a strong spiritual streak and includes prayer in her nightly preparation. In fact, she found that playing Vivian was exhilarating. Formerly very attached to her wavy blonde tresses, she shaved her head for the role and said in interviews that she preferred not to wear a cap in public but rather to experience the sensation of baldness fully.

"People say, 'Don't you carry this with you?'" she told me. Her answer: "No, if there's an issue it brings up for me in my life, I look at it. I have a lot to deal with in relation to death . . . my own fears of death, wanting to confront that more. Every character you play can help you got through something in life. It doesn't make me feel depressed, it makes me thrilled."

It seems to work that way for audiences too: Light got letters from audience members who survived cancer and said that *Wit* changed their lives. For actors, I guess there isn't any better proof that you're working the right way.

Chapter 9

TOUCH OF EVIL:
PLAYING VILLAINS

In an interview, British actor Brenda Blethyn once said, "Normally we actors like to play nice people that audiences like."

Well, maybe. In any case, Blethyn succeeded in making her shrill, boozy harridan (in *Little Voice*) believable, even sympathetic, if not actually likable.

What is the trick to making an unreconstructed villain fully dimensional? Because of course in most cases that's what we desire: to play our roles with depth. Before Shakespeare's day, as Shakespearean actor Morris Carnovsky points out in his book *The Actor's Eye*, the morality plays assigned only one quality to a character: lechery, sloth, etc. Shakespeare changed all that. Think of Anthony Hopkins' meanie for the ages, the coldly intellectual Hannibal Lecter in the film *Silence of the Lambs*, and Hopkins' equally creepy yet tormented on-screen Richard Nixon, two undeniably multidimensional characters.

There are two key elements to playing evil. One is to "Look for goodness," according to the Russian master, Constantin Stanislavski, as his disciple Sonia Moore reports in *The Stanislavski Method*. "Trying to project only evil would make the performance heavy and monotonous," he warned.

The other is to justify the evil actions. Shakespeare tends to provide all the justification you need.

I called one of Oregon Shakespeare Festival's Iagos, Anthony Heald, to find out how he went about creating one of the Bard's arch villains. Heald has in fact played a variety of nasty types in his career, including the smarmy Dr. Chilton in *Silence of the Lambs*, who establishes his despicable character right off the bat by trying to put the make on Jodie Foster. Heald said he's drawn to the complexities contained in characters with a dark side; his "hope-to-play" list included Richard III and Claudius as well as Iago.

"I asked a director friend of mine, 'What's the secret?'" said Heald. "He said, 'Iago loves Othello, even in the worst of it.' I used that as a springboard. Iago's primary opponent is Desdemona, so he can get Othello back. That way, I see him as a person I can understand.

"And I also decided," continued Heald, "he's not sociopathic but narcissistic. Things need to coincide with his interests or he becomes frustrated and enraged. He has very negative feelings toward women and other people that he dislikes. In battle he can exorcise those feelings. But after nine months in Venice, away from the field [a given circumstance provided by Shakespeare], he has all these feelings bottled up."

In order to stay focused on Iago's human qualities, Heald said he tried to ban the word *evil* from the rehearsal hall. "Evil people do what they do because they need to in order to get what they need. What they need is, in their own eyes, good. If they have to do evil things to achieve that . . . well, that's no worse than cardinals blessing the troops!" He added, "One of the things that makes playing an evil character like Iago so interesting is that he behaves one way and is perceived another way, so you get to play the mask and the face underneath. When you're playing a good character, it's hard to play any negative qualities. I find there's so much more variety and opportunity when you're playing a darker character."

I asked Heald if it's hard to find personal ways to identify with bad characters. "I use Stanislavski's 'magic if,'" he said. "I have to start from myself. That's the only resource I have."

Sonia Moore writes about the usefulness of the magic if, in which the actor improvisationally explores what he or she would do in the character's situation: "*If* is a supposition and it does not imply or assert anything that exists. It helps one to think of something that *could* exist," writes Moore. "*If* is a powerful stimulus to the imagination, thoughts, and emotions."

If you simply can't imagine yourself doing evil deeds under any circumstances, you may be lying to yourself. Think about your relationships with employers, colleagues, family members, friends, that obnoxious next-door neighbor. Think about your childhood misbehavior (sure, you were a kid, but you were still *you*). Have you never in your life been manipulative, selfish, mean-spirited? Don't place yourself above your characters—none of us are lily-white pure.

Heald also looked for Iago's virtues: "He's brave, audacious, improvisational, a brilliant tactician," said Heald. Similarly, to play Perry, an "acid-tongued racist," in Terrence McNally's *Love! Valour! Compassion!* Heald looked for moments of tenderness to make him a rounder character and to put the negative qualities into greater contrast. "You have to find ways to open up an audience so you can punch them in the gut," explained Heald. "With any character, you're looking for a way to keep the audience surprised and to fill the role with as many colors as possible. You don't want to play one note all through."

In fact, in order to surprise the audience, Heald convinced *Othello* director Tony Taccone to let him add what he calls a silent "manufactured moment" to a crucial scene. In Act IV, Scene II, just after the two-faced Iago has comforted a distraught Desdemona (who is then led away by Emilia), he turns to the audience. "They expect I'll say something biting and acid, and I don't. I kind of freeze and open my mouth and sink into a chair. It's a glimpse inside Iago of something we haven't seen, a sense of awareness of the consequences of what he's doing. Audiences have said they felt complicit. I try to take them in as co-conspirators. That's delicious."

Just as you want to avoid heavy-handed villainy, you also don't want to whitewash your character. I've seen good actors so busy justifying the bad and dredging up the good that their character appears wishy-washy. As Brenda Blethyn says, perhaps it has to do with our innate need to be liked by the audience. After all, none of us goes into the profession in order to be hated! But as Heald pointed out, "It's always a trap for actors to think about how they're perceived by the audience. You have to be concerned with an objective, with what the character needs, not with what *you* need."

English actor Norman Rodway, a 70-year-old Royal Shakespeare Company veteran, played the quintessential creep, Hitler, on film in the offbeat, part fantasy, part psychological drama *The Empty Mirror*. He commented, "With all characters, good or bad, you always have to play them from their own point of view" and ignore what anybody else says about them. Once cast, he found he had no time to do research; he played his Hitler as written, "a man who's trying to justify himself all the time. He's not acknowledging his evilness."

He added, "I think it's always a great error to look for sympathy from the audience. I've seen actors so desperate to be liked that they butter up what they're doing." He noted that characters like Richard III, and Edmond in *King Lear*, both of whom he's played, inform the audience right away that they are evil, and that's that. But Rodway's Hitler, unlike the Shakespearean scoundrels he's played, is an ordinary guy who "just says it as he sees it."

Michael Chekhov writes, in *On the Technique of Acting*, "I observed the psychology of an actor who was constantly drawn to evil, negative characters. Strangely enough, the more expressively he performed them, the more sympathetic they became, remaining nevertheless unmistakably evil." To achieve that elusive dichotomy is surely what we all hope for in portraying stage and screen monsters.

Chapter 10

PLAYING MENTALLY CHALLENGED

Mentally handicapped people—those with a subnormal level of intelligence, whatever the cause—are an integral part of the lives of many of us, myself included. And the concerns of a society increasingly sensitive to "otherness" are reflected in our popular culture: more (and more fully developed) characters with mental limitations are showing up in film, TV, and theatre. In 1968, Cliff Robertson played a mentally handicapped man in the film *Charly* (based on the short story "Flowers for Algernon"). Later, Larry Drake was Benny in the TV series *L.A. Law,* with Amanda Plummer as his similarly handicapped girlfriend, and Dustin Hoffman was the autistic Raymond in *Rain Man.* Then there were, among others, Tom Hanks as Forrest Gump, Juliette Lewis in *The Other Sister,* Sean Penn in *I Am Sam.* Actors seem to relish these roles—what male doesn't want to play Lenny in *Of Mice and Men?*—and I don't remember ever seeing an actor do a poor job playing such a person. It seems there's something inspiring about the challenge.

When a Hollywood group staged *The Boys Next Door,* Tom Griffin's 1986 play (and a TV movie in 1996, with Nathan Lane and Mare Winningham) about a group of mentally challenged adults setting up house together in an attempt to mainstream into society, I gave one of the producers a call. Grinnell Morris, who is also a cast member, told me he grew up with a severely mentally disabled sister (who's now 31) and insisted that the cast spend some time with residents of the Burbank Center of the Retarded. The cast bowled several times with the residents, went to two dances, and just hung out. I asked him what they learned and how he created his character.

We discussed some general facts about the developmentally disabled, all of which provide opportunities for actors to make creative and varied choices:

1. Some know they are "retarded," others don't, depending on their level of intelligence.

2. Their preoccupations are usually specific and simple. For Morris' sister it's food, dogs, and music: "When are we going to eat? When are we going to see a dog?" For Morris' character, Norman, who's mid-range disabled, he chose keys ("because they make me important"), donuts (Norman works in a donut shop), and his girlfriend, Sheila.

3. They may have some distortion with their mouth that causes them to slur their words. For some, it's a mental barrier; for others, it's at least partly physical—their hard or soft palates may be misshapen. "You never want to play the impediment; you want to overcome it," cautioned Morris. "If I loosen my jaw and then try to speak clearly, that's the most I can do."

4. For most, good posture is not a high priority.

5. Many have various physical disabilities and ailments.

6. They usually physicalize more impulsively than do those with normal mental capacity. "Expression coming out through the extremities is common," said Morris. "They may clench their hands, flick their fingers—nerves and tension are not repressed."

7. Although Down's syndrome has a distinctive look, many other types of "retarded" people look normal.

Said Morris, "It's a matter of first understanding retardation as a whole and what that means in a very holistic way, then making it specific. What makes Norman Norman and not just a generic retarded person?"

He mentioned two acting traps. One is playing stupid or crazy. Mentally handicapped people have the exact same feelings and needs as anyone else; they just have a different way of expressing themselves, and a harder time communicating.

The other trap concerns motivation. "As actors, we say, why am I saying this line?" noted Morris. "But retarded people don't necessarily get motivated the same way we do. Norman has a line: 'This is a good song. It's got a beat. I wouldn't go to no dance where they didn't have popcorn.' For Norman there's no transition. If he's excited about one thing, he just goes right on to the next thing he's excited about." On the other hand, there are times when you want to take extra-slow transitions, because your character can't think very fast. "It's about trying to justify the behavior but not necessarily understand it on a logical level," Morris explained.

He elaborated further: "I have the capacity to communicate and get what I want. So you'd think retarded people would be frustrated [because they have to struggle to communicate]. But because they've been that way all their life, it's part of who they are. I don't think they feel frustration more than anyone else. It's like someone who's been blind all their life. They are just who they are. That's one of the most refreshing things about retarded people—no bones, no games, no anything. Even if they're trying to manipulate a situation, you can see it so clearly. It's a pure, simple innocent condition. You peel away layers of things that society builds into all of us and you see more clearly what the human spirit is about."

In *The Boys Next Door,* coproducer William Dennis Hurley played Arnold, whom he described as marginally retarded with a depressive personality. Hurley did just what he does with any character: He looked for qualities in himself that matched Arnold's. "He's hyperactive, a compulsive chatterer, a ringleader. I'm definitely a ringleader. Like Arnold, I always want to know what's going on, what others are thinking. . . . I found out what parts of me I could bring to a non-normal-functioning character."

He also made sure he understood what was wrong with Arnold clinically and therefore what Arnold's limitations and possibilities would be. The challenge, he said, was finding appropriate forms of expression. "I had to question everything: Would I pick up the book this way? Would I go into the bedroom like that? At the beginning it's incredible analysis of the behavior to be sure it's truthful to the mental capacity." Such intense scrutiny can make it hard for an actor to be present in the moment in rehearsals; so at a certain point Hurley gave over that function to the director.

"Basically, you play a retarded character the same way you'd play a character with an accent, or an impediment of some kind," he said. "You learn it, you let it be second nature, then you stop thinking about it. You establish the issues and then proceed as if they weren't issues."

Stephanie Hunt, who played the slightly mentally challanged Rose Mundy in *Dancing at Lughnasa* at Berkeley Repertory Theatre, made the decision, after consulting medical dictionaries, that her character had suffered oxygen deprivation at birth. She spent some time at a center where mentally handicapped people worked; spent an evening with a woman and her handicapped sister; and went to the mall with a teenager and her handicapped friend. "They lent me her diary, so I got to see her repetitive thoughts," Hunt told me. "The director told me to watch children, but there's something different. I felt Rose had a gleam in her eye. She had secrets." She added, "It's like any role. You always have to think, what does that character want and how do they get it?"

She also noted that it's important to analyze the script: What function within the play is this character serving? "I think retarded characters serve to provide a different perspective. I found that to play Rose I really had to open myself up, do lots of sensory work, mental imagery, extensive warm-ups. Everyone knows someone with too few inhibitions. That's what she's like. And she'd pick up on other people's feelings and transmit them, like an emotional antenna." Physically, Hunt let her mouth hang open a lot: "I think that's the most clichéd thing I did."

All three actors mentioned the particular joy of playing mentally handicapped characters. For Hurley, the experience reminded him that no matter what role he's playing, the most important thing to focus on is what's inside.

"Retarded characters bring their own reality onstage, their own rules," observed Hunt. For her, playing Rose Mundy was an opportunity to extend herself creatively.

"Everyone at some point in their career should try it, even just a scene in acting class," said Morris. "It's very liberating. Here's the reality of playing a character with a much narrower frame of reference than you: It's part of your ability to play pretend as an actor. Which is something I love to do. There's a huge kid in all of us."

A final comment: I believe that producers and directors have a responsibility to look for physically handicapped actors when roles call for such handicaps. Should the same ethic apply when casting the mentally handicapped? A few years ago the TV series *Life Goes On* hired Chris Burke, a mildly mentally handicapped actor, for a major role, and audiences accepted the show for its verisimilitude, although Burke's acting skills weren't up to the level of the rest of the cast. I have to say I agree with Grinnell Morris, who said he thinks the best way we can get an insight into people with subnormal intelligence is to see really good actors portray them.

Chapter 11

AGING GRACEFULLY

When you're required to age over the course of a single performance—say your character progresses from her twenties to fifties or sixties, à là *Same Time Next Year*—the temptation is to rely on a combination of makeup, costume, and certain physical traits: the wide-eyed naïveté of youth versus the bobbly-headed querulousness of seniority. Sure, there are certain attributes and physical characteristics that are rightfully associated with certain age groups: most younger people *are* bouncier, most older people *do* seem stiffer. I know I get up from the couch more carefully now that I'm fifty—er, something, and my voice is deeper. And as we go into our, ahem, twilight years, we do tend to slump from osteoporosis. But as in all aspects of the craft of acting, you want to avoid the generic and focus on the specific and the personal. Here's how:

1. *Create a history.* As Los Angeles acting teacher Judith Weston pointed out, no matter what your character's various ages, she needs an overall spine across the arc of the play. Create that superobjective by inventing a complete history for your character to add to the information in the text. (Many professionals feel that creating this type of biography is a waste of time, but in the case of a character who ages before our eyes, it really is needed.) Fine-tune that history by adding on layers of experience—career problems, child-rearing challenges, heartbreaks—as your character matures. You can also work on mini-objectives for each age and stage of your character's development, as her needs and perspectives change. This strictly interior homework and rehearsal work is not something you'll consciously use in performance, but it will affect you.

2. *Do general research.* To go older, you could talk to a doctor about the various infirmities of age, hang out with older relatives, watch elderly people on buses, on park benches, in the supermarket, in a senior community center. Here are some physical possibilities to consider.

As we grow older, the tissue between the disks of our spine actually compresses, becomes less spongy, so we shrink. Many of us get arthritis, which causes us to lose flexibility; our joints stiffen; maybe we can't rotate our necks as far. Or we develop bunions, so our feet hurt. Perhaps our back aches. We have a fear of falling and breaking our brittle bones, so we may stand with our feet planted more widely apart. Maybe we have shortness of breath (imagine your character to be a lifetime smoker), or a reluctance to squander our energy. Our voices may get lower as we mature, then higher later. We get near-sighted, or our hearing isn't as acute. Vanessa Redgrave is said to have settled upon merely squinting to convey an aging Isadora Duncan in the 1968 film *Isadora*. Also, as Uta Hagen points out in *Respect for Acting*, we develop an anxiety and protectiveness about our specific condition.

3. *Look within.* One actor in her forties taps into her own knowledge of growing older and uses her imagination to take it a few steps further. You can do that at any age. Another actor likes to remember times when he had physical problems. When he broke his leg, he walked with a limp, and the sense memory of that time helps him when playing older characters.

4. *Be specific and don't "indicate."* Weston suggested choosing one or two specific physical adjustments for age. "Don't try to *play* ten years older or forty years older than you are," she cautioned. "Break it down to a specific task." For older: Maybe you have stiffness or pain in your right knee and your left wrist, that's all; don't try to show it to the audience, just feel it. Another teacher noted that the given circumstances of the play may affect your choices: Does your character live in a cold climate? His arthritis might flare up. Has he been a laborer for many years, with an accumulation of job-related injuries that affect his posture and flexibility? One teacher added, "As the body ages, it takes on the history of the person." She believes that you can achieve that organic process intuitively by exploring your character in depth in rehearsals.

5. *Use tricks.* An actor, playing a woman who ages several years in *Kindertransport,* removed her bra (under her shirt) to portray the older version of the character, so she could get that saggy, weighed-down-by-gravity feeling. Another suggested imagining that you're wearing a piece of clothing that has personal meaning and, for you, connotes a particular age.

6. *Avoid traps.* When going old, said one director, actors tend to play too old. Another common mistake is to rely too heavily on the physical and neglect the internal work. And of course it's important to avoid clichés: old people are not always creaky and crotchety, or even cute. Everybody's different. Also, as one teacher noted, the danger at either end of the age scale is "commenting" on your character—consciously or unconsciously making fun of them. Finally, as Hagen in her infinite wisdom and common sense points out, there's not much difference in how you feel or look between your twenties and your forties, especially across the footlights or filmed through filters.

In other words, don't overdo it. Less is more.

Chapter 12

PLAYING CHILDREN

"Actors probably owe most of their skills to that devastatingly narcissistic 'Look at me!' which keeps the majority of them still embroiled in an emotional adolescence."

That charming sentiment was expressed by the late British writer Dennis Potter in the intro to his TV play *Blue Remembered Hills*. He also stipulated that all the roles in the play—seven seven-year-olds—be played by adults, so that the audience wouldn't be tempted to sentimentalize the notion of childhood.

That stipulation makes sense for his play, which explores the dark side of childhood innocence during wartime. He wrote that he did not want "an indulgent 'Ah!' of softened retrospective to interfere with the sight of two little girls playing with a china doll, or four little boys deciding that, after all, there was nothing better than a box of matches for setting light to something."

Clive Chafer, a British-born actor and director, says there's a lot of truth in what the apparently crotchety Potter wrote.

"For every actor, part of staying open and flexible is staying childlike in your acceptance of what comes your way," commented Chafer. "If you can be as open as a seven-year-old to the stimuli you're given by others, your response will be fuller. Improv work is based on saying yes to what comes your way, like children. So in some ways you're just asking actors to be actors. . . . In New Age speak, you're asking them to get in touch with their inner child, which many actors have not lost touch with."

When he directed *Blue Remembered Hills,* his cast rehearsed by visiting Sunday school groups, classrooms, and playgrounds. Because children play differently when adults are around, the cast actually spied on the little buggers. "They're loose-limbed . . . not terribly coordinated, although some are showing signs of coordination. Some use their muscles well in throwing a ball, others don't. It's important to observe the exact age," he added.

There are traps in playing children, though: "You've got to make your physicality pay off for the action and the character," said Chafer. "There's nothing gratuitous. The changes can be 180 degrees, but they have to be fully embodied and rooted in some action called for by the script. As soon as the actors start to lose that, it's 'Hey, look, I'm playing a seven-year-old!' The audience will be interested for about five minutes . . . We have to get seven-year-oldness focused into what's happening in the script. If the actors are specific about what that child wants in every moment, which can change from one half-sentence to the next, it'll seem a lot like seven-year-olds. To us it seems like they're 150 percent in that emotional moment."

Sheila Balter played the role of an outspoken nine-year-old for several years in a row in a holiday production of a dramatization of Grace Paley's short story "The Loudest Voice." She attributes her authenticity to an artist-in-residence gig working with third, fourth, and fifth graders in an after-school program. She modeled schoolgirl Shirley after one of her students, a particularly bright girl with strong opinions. "She had an openness and a forthrightness that you have then; she felt free to express herself unencumbered by self-consciousness," explained Balter.

Balter carefully observed how kids walk and stand and behave. "The key for me was physical," she said. "I chose a few things: Something as simple as bending one knee, putting my weight on the other leg . . . I wanted the sleeves of my sweater to be long so I could play with the cuffs. And kids kind of drag their feet a little bit."

She also incorporated specific memories from her own childhood: Recalling a favorite teacher, she chose to have a crush on the schoolteacher in the play.

"I've learned over the years of doing this play that simpler is better," she said. "I used to have her a little more hunched over, trying to make myself smaller physically, more coy. I tried out some squirming and wiggling and twisting of my arms. I think I've toned down some of the physical things. That's really not necessary. It's the same as any acting: It has to be truly coming from you internally. If you're trying to act cute, it doesn't work, as a child or as an adult. It's not about imitating their voice; I'm probably a little more in my chest and head voice as opposed to my lower register, but it's still my voice. It's about running and springing and finding, going back to your own childish spirit. Remembering your relationship to the other kids. Curiosity and wonder are key elements, too. . . . I try to be very present at every moment, because for children every moment is really an adventure."

Carol Hazenfield, an improv performer who has taught improv and scripted theatre in San Francisco, made several important points:

- Children's responses are more primitive than ours. A normal, healthy child, up to the age of eleven or twelve (when self-consciousness kicks in), will let any emotion out.

- Children are physically less controlled because they don't have the motor skills we have.

- "No children I know," said Hazenfield, "stand with their toes turned in and acting cutesie. Adult actors do that. It's one of my pet peeves." Mine, too.

- Actors tend to go for result; rather than play a specific child, they play a generality. If you're paying the same kind of detailed attention to character in playing a child as in playing an adult, you'll get a whole range of specifiers—weight, shyness, clumsiness, extroversion versus introversion; all the characteristics of human behavior are present in both adults and children.

- Another, opposite trap: playing children as too self-aware. Clues: if your emotional choices or objectives are too complex. Better to choose more primal objectives and responses.

- Real kids won't stop playing their objective till they're shut down totally. They want what they want and they want it now and make direct tactical choices to get it—they wheedle, cry, dance, and flirt, and they can turn on a dime. As adults, we tend to not allow ourselves to be that emotionally invested—"probably," said Hazenfield, "because we have a genetic memory of how painful it is to be a child." She added, "But the actor's job, whether playing an adult or child, is to open oneself to hope and assume your character will succeed, and take your lumps if the outcome doesn't go your way."

- Unlike adults, children can forget their previous emotion. When playing an adult, you always have to bring the baggage from the last emotional moment to the next, right? But when playing a kid, you don't have to. This awareness of real-time transactions should affect all your choices: physical, vocal, etc.

A few other tips:

- Young people always want to seem older. If you can layer an effort to be sophisticated on top of a youthful sensibility, that's a good thing.

- We've all been young. Depending on the demands of the text, you can create a sense memory or affective memory to remember how insecure you felt, to remember a time when you were impulsive, even rash.

- Try creating a lightness in your pelvis and in your shoulders.

"The nature of playing children is they don't know the rules yet," explained Hazenfield. "They haven't had enough trial and error to know what will work or not work. There's a lack of cynicism. So if they get their objective they tend to celebrate and be more delighted, and if they don't get it they are crushed. There's an emotional investment."

So—did the actors who played seven-year-olds in *Blue Remembered Hills* pull it off? Partly. There were some physical clichés that didn't work: self-conscious pigeon-toed stances, kicking the dirt sheepishly with the toe of a shoe, too much generalized fidgeting and flinging around of bodies. Sheila Balter is right: Less is more. On the other hand, the commitment to objectives was, as Clive Chafer suggested, 150 percent. And as Hazenfield mentioned, every character rejoiced boldly in every objective accomplished. And despite the flaws, by midway into the play, my companion and I agreed: Our brains had totally accepted the fact that these were children romping before us. Which means you don't have to push; you can trust the audience to get it.

Finally, as Hazenfield observed, playing a child can help you get over some of your misconceptions about how adults behave. "A lot of bad acting comes from a 'that's not logical, my character wouldn't say that' mentality," said Hazenfield. That way lies cookie-cutter acting. Getting into the mind of a child can free your imagination in a way that works for adult characters as well.

Chapter 13

SOCIAL CLASSES

As actors, we are often called upon to play characters who belong to particular and extreme social classes: upper (e.g., Shakespearean royalty; European or East Coast old-money aristocrats) or lower (the so-called working classes; "trailer trash"; the down and out). Yet many of us probably come from within the ranks of the American middle classes. Question: What do we need to know about playing a social class different than our own in order to avoid stereotypes, clichés, or condescension? The answer appears at the end of this chapter. In the meantime, let me share with you some free-ranging discussions I had on this somewhat elusive topic with a few actors whose work I greatly respect.

John Spencer, chatting on the phone from his trailer on the set of *The West Wing*, reminded me that Lee Strasberg used to say that the audience doesn't necessarily know the king is a king from his behavior. More important is how the *other* characters are treating him. Strasberg's observation is a good reminder of the importance of deep listening and reacting. "Assumptions of how a king would behave could lead to posturing," warned Spencer in his familiar, gravelly voice. "How the hell do you know how a king would behave? The grounding of an actor in a role is understanding the *human* behavior. The other things are accoutrements."

Spencer comes from a blue collar New Jersey background but obviously can play a range of characters—in *The West Wing* he's the president's chief of staff. When he first read for the show, the producers loved what he did because he played the chief of staff as if he were coach for the Yankees. "That was not necessarily my intention," laughed Spencer. "There is so much about this man who is so educated and eclectic. He's a lawyer, a great team player, a great motivator. So I tried to bring that kind of gruff, baser note to the role, if that doesn't sound too pretentious.

"Tommy Mullaney (in *L.A. Law*) and I shared similar character traits.

He was streetwise. I'm streetwise." Spencer's Mullaney was a brilliant lawyer with a working-class sensibility.

When I asked Spencer to name a character he's played who is quite *unlike* him, he mentioned classical plays in regional theatre, particularly Shakespeare. "That's where I can believe that research can be very helpful," he said. He reads about the period he's depicting: "I'm interested in how they went to the bathroom, what they ate—little, active things that I draw from research that can affect my behavior are very useful."

Surprisingly he also mentioned, as another role that's far from himself, Mark in Emily Mann's play *Still Life*—a character who is, in fact, working class. Yet Mark is a Vietnam vet, and Spencer himself has never been to war. So the working-class background that Spencer shares with Mark was not necessarily an important tool in developing the role.

In fact, your own social-class background can affect you any which way in terms of your natural affinity and the way you're perceived by casting directors. For example, dark and hulking American Conservatory Theater actor Marco Barricelli comes from a highly educated family—both his parents were Ivy League graduates and educators—yet his strongest inclination is toward working-class characters: Mangiacavallo in *The Rose Tattoo*, Stanley in *A Streetcar Named Desire*. "Go figure," he said.

On the other hand, Dennis Franz, who has created the memorable, lower-class character Sipowicz in *NYPD Blue*, is first generation American, his father a baker and his mother a postal worker. Which may or may not have given him an edge in crafting his police detective character.

Petite, blonde Lorri Holt is often told she looks aristocratic, but she's from a Midwestern working class/farm background and identifies with lower-class types, although she's been cast at both ends of the social spectrum. Certain aspects of upper-middle to upper-class sensibility do feel natural to her ("My mother always told me I was born with a silver spoon in my mouth!" she laughed), but when she played, for example, wealthy Scilla in Caryl Churchill's *Serious Money* at Berkeley Repertory Theatre, she had to work hard to identify with Scilla's feeling of entitlement.

Like Holt, Robert Ernst, whose voice is even gravelly-er than Spencer's, comes from a rural background. The nearest town was 10 miles away, population: 300. "The condition I was raised in no longer exists," said Ernst. "In an urban environment it would be considered poor white trash. We might have been considered lower middle-class at the time, that is, we had indoor bathrooms but weren't rich. We were like share croppers." His father died of overwork at age thirty-eight. Ernst's movie and TV roles tend to be "deranged guys, cops, crazy guys, poor guys, rednecks, or white trash." The biggest stretch for him was playing Wiley in Marlane Meyer's *Kingfish* at San Francisco's Magic Theatre—an upper-class gay man. "His sense of grace, his assumptions, were different," said Ernst.

On the other hand, when he appeared in Athol Fugard's *Playland,* he also had to work hard to identify with the character—because although the character was working class, he was a South African racist. So in that case, social class had relatively little bearing on Ernst's bonding with the character. "I had to draw on the pains and guilt this guy suffered," he explained. On the other end of the social scale, he played an upper-class executive in Sam Shepard's *Eyes for Consuela*—and that character, too, was racist, although more covertly. Ernst had to dig deep for "a place in me that can present that sense of righteousness as a viable argument. He was used to having his shoes shined, being driven to work."

So we see that social class is only one of many factors to be considered when playing a character, and certainly not the most important. Even if a character is from your own social background, he or she could be different from you in very basic ways. And as with any role of whatever class or milieu, you have to find a way to identify with your character. Bob Ernst reminded me of the adage that you don't need to like your character, but you do have to love him or her.

I was eager to talk to Velina Brown and her husband, Michael Sullivan, because both are longtime actors with the agit-prop San Francisco Mime Troupe, a collective that creates original material from a social-political perspective. Social class is something that's discussed during rehearsals for every Mime Troupe play.

Brown, from a middle-class, African-American background (both parents grew up poor in the South but are college grads) and, casting-wise, perceived as "elegant," has the skill to succeed with a variety of roles. Playing a bag lady, she focused on her character's situation, and that helped her make a lot of physical choices. "As a woman living on the street, you have to play down your womanness so people won't take advantage of you," she said. "You might take a certain posture, standing with your legs apart, a fighting stance." On the other hand, to play an upper-class twit, she thinks about how she'd expect people to react to her. "The higher up you are the softer you can speak."

But mostly, in plays and film, she gets cast as educated types, often as a nurse, which is her mother's profession. "I think of class as having different components: education, income, and also frame of mind," she said. "There are people who don't have much money, but the way they carry themselves and live their lives conveys a feeling of freedom and options. A person who makes six figures might feel very confined in their work, afraid of being downsized, so that person's mentality would be 'poor.'"

Regarding physicality, Michael Sullivan, when playing a homeless man, chose to assume a regal posture. He felt the character saw himself not as pathetic but as a pioneer among street entrepreneurs. "Wealthy people can look like the homeless, physically—crumbling under the burden of life," he pointed out. "You can play the kind of wealthy person who slinks into a room and stands in a corner. The class stuff is internal when it comes to physicalization—it has to do with a particular person's response to his circumstances." The Mime Troupe, he noted, works in physical archetypes but never in physical clichés. There's a subtle difference.

Let's talk about clichés. Clichés can go in any direction. Lower-class types can be played as pro forma doofuses (stupid rather than merely uneducated), or, as Sullivan observed, as idiot savants. "Just because you're homeless doesn't mean you're Socrates," he said, "or because you're a union member in Flint, Michigan, that you're Eugene Debs." Also, because you're rich doesn't mean you're snooty. Some of these clichés appear in the writing, like the proverbial hooker-with-a-heart-of-gold, or the tobacco-chewing farmer with a *Deliverance* mentality. (Interestingly, *San Francisco Chronicle* movie critic Mick LaSalle noted a recent trend in film scripts to present villains as posh Brits, speaking the queen's English—a sort of reverse snobbism. "There's a kneejerk class hostility at work here," he wrote, "and also an antagonism toward intellectuals. The villains talk in a way that suggests people who have spent a lot of time alone, reading dangerous books.") But whatever the flaws in the writing, it behooves the actor to struggle mightily against a simplistic, one-dimensional characterization. Said Holt, "Everyone has multiple facets. Your job is to show the dimensions of the character."

So we're all agreed: no clichés. Fine. How to avoid them? The usual way: Look for the complexities within the character, be specific, and personalize. Is there a grain of truth in stereotypes? Yes, said Holt, but you have to find whatever grain of truth works for you, and then particularize. Here are a few general guidelines:

Don't make assumptions. "There are as many dull, stupid upper-class people as intelligent, sensitive lower-class people," said Holt. "Don't take the easy road . . . avoid sentimentality." Cautioned John Spencer, "Don't play any preconceived concept of how the character would or should behave; look to the human being first, his needs, his past experience. I'm sure Queen Elizabeth doesn't go around every minute of the day thinking, I'm a queen, I'm behaving like a queen. She's a woman who's concerned about her children, who may not like the way she looks in a certain dress."

Said Ernst, "I've had a few occasions to play farmers or rural types in movies. All chew tobacco, are out of *Deliverance,* are considered in that vicinity to be a genius if they have an IQ of 72. But I had an uncle considered retarded, and when he died it turns out he'd been playing the stock market for years. He had a speech impediment, was shy, and was known as the most loving and generous uncle. Imagine everyone's surprise! I see actors making assumptions—equating money and intelligence."

Play the situation. In her role as Queen Clytemnestra in *Iphigenia at the Bay of Aulis,* Brown focused on the character's need to save her daughter's life. "Being a queen didn't help Clytemnestra," she noted.

Don't condescend. As a young actress, Brown played a black South African woman in Salaelo Maredi's *Homeland.* Her character's situation seemed so desperate that Brown's own middle-class American feelings of empathy bled over. The director, a South African, told her that she was playing her character as pitiful. "These people actually do laugh, they do have a life," he scolded her.

Be specific. Depending on your character's class, the kind of everyday activities common to that class may affect his or her physical posture, attitudes, demeanor. "What does that character eat?" said Spencer. "What kind of restaurants does he go to? What kind of clothes does he wear? Look for things you can use. If he works construction, using a drill hammer every day, that may affect his arms and shoulder, make him slump. And the rest should follow."

Focus on your actions and objectives. Marco Barricelli, who approaches every character, whether it's Prince Hamlet or Stanley Kowalski—or, in one case, God—the exact same way, said, "Look for clues in the language. . . . Class distinction is less useful in the process of building a character than are the basics: What do I need, what do I want, how do I get it, what are my obstacles?" I think that's it in a nutshell, folks.

Chapter 14

ANIMALS

In one busy play-going period, I saw four plays with animals in them, which made me wonder how actors can work most effectively with furry, four-footed colleagues.

In an outdoor production of *Henry IV, Part I*, the husband and wife playing Hotspur and Lady Hotspur brought in their own bright-eyed, heart-meltingly cute new pup for a scene. In another al fresco Shakespeare, *Love's Labour's Lost,* on a grassy outdoor set, Emily Ackerman and Colman Domingo (as a pair of rustics) shared the stage at times with a balky pygmy goat named Pepsi and her more docile understudy, 7-Up. Yet a third open-air production, *Mountain Days, the John Muir Musical,* included three different horses plus wagons and handlers. And in *Frank Loesser's Hans Christian Andersen*, director Martha Clarke, who originally wanted a monkey, two doves, chickens, and a flock of ducks, settled for a 65-pound Staffordshire terrier named Hedley. "I always have animals if I can, it's good for the spirit," Clarke told me. She travels with her two Pomeranians.

Here are a few helpful hints for acting with our fuzzy friends.

Lesson #1: Learn their toilet habits.

This is a primary concern for actor, handler, director, and audience alike. Worst case example: At a performance of *Fiddler on the Roof* atop Mt. Tamalpais in Marin County once, Tevye's cow dumped on his shoe during the poignant last scene. Oy. On the other hand, the horses that director Rich Elliott hired from a local family for *John Muir* came outfitted, thankfully, with equine diapers. During *Love's Labour's,* Ackerman and two other actors were on poop detail. Ackerman made her entrances with a bucket and broom. She discovered early on that the goats liked to mark their territory at a particular place backstage, so she'd make a regular pit stop there before entering.

Of course, there are unpredictable moments, and East Coast–based Bill Berloni, who has been providing animals for film, Broadway, and regional theatre for the past twenty-five years (including the dog for *Hans Christian*

Andersen), has seen them all. In a production of *Annie,* he watched from the wings as the dog Sandy began to get sick, and frantically snapped his fingers at the onstage Annie to let the dog come to him. But Annie grabbed Sandy to keep him onstage, and Sandy barfed—just as she launched into "Tomorrow."

Lesson #2: Bond.

Another big concern is to get the animal relaxed and familiar with you. Ackerman and Domingo were the only cast members to feed, pet, and walk the goats. In fact, when the creatures were first delivered by a local farmer, Ackerman promptly crawled into the cage with the nanny goat, "because she was freaked out and I needed to bond." Maybe it helped that Ackerman was raised on a farm "with gigantic, horrible goats."

Ackerman noted that Pepsi and 7-Up didn't arrive until tech rehearsals, and it would have been much better to have them earlier in the process. An animal needs time to get used to your voice, and you need time to learn its habits from the handler.

A caveat, though: Not all animals will react well to your invading their personal space.

Lesson #3: Allow time for them to get used to your costume.

Colman Domingo worked with a dog in a modernized *Two Gentlemen of Verona* once, and when the mutt first saw Domingo in his radical bike messenger outfit, he snarled. On the other hand, Ackerman's goat grew to love her period attire.

Lesson #4: Pack snacks.

Ackerman kept grain, popcorn, apples in her pockets, especially important for goats, who will notoriously eat anything, including the set. Some dogs like biscuits. Find out your costar's culinary preferences, and reward, reward, reward.

Lesson #5: Be consistent, patient, and kind.

Sounds like a no-brainer, but apparently not. Bill Berloni said that actors sometimes get angry when animals make mistakes. "It's often, 'The dog's upstaging my scene' attitude," he told me, "which creates an animosity that continues to snowball." He added, "The biggest human misconception is that a trained dog doesn't need rehearsal or patience. Everyone gets wrapped up in the show and neglects the dog and wonders why it doesn't perform. Animals don't have the capacity for cognitive thought. They learn and respond by repetition and patience."

Berloni also pointed out that every species, and every animal within every species, has different requirements. How physically close you get to it, what it likes for rewards (a biscuit, a toy, a snuggle) can vary. Ask the handler.

Lesson #6: Go with the flow.

This is a biggie. We all know that animals can upstage us without half trying. How do we deal with it?

Said Berloni, "Animals are more consistent than actors. They're so motivated by positive reinforcements. If they get a command they understand and know there's a reward, they're enthusiastic. But what happens is, someone doesn't give them a command properly, or the stage manager is talking too loudly offstage, or someone in the front row is eating a candy bar, and the animal gets distracted." Part of Berloni's job is to train actors to recognize—by, say, the flick of a canine ear—if Rover's attention is wandering, and to refocus him.

But if you can't refocus the animal quickly enough, and often even if you can, you're still likely to be upstaged. "If actors are doing a scene with an animal and the audience laughs, the animal will look at where the noise is coming from, and it looks like the animal is mugging," explained Berloni. "It breaks the fourth wall. So the audience laughs more. This happens all the time until the animal gets used to the fact that the audience is going to make this noise. Don't fight it. You'll lose. You have to ad lib, look at the audience and shrug. Then you're in on the joke with the audience as opposed to being the butt of the joke."

It's hard to imagine this could work in a serious piece, but on the other hand, what are the alternatives? "If it's you and an animal on stage, never fight the animal," agreed Domingo. "Throw focus there and you'll have a better show."

Lesson #7: Stay flexible and aware.

This is similar to Lesson #6. Ackerman discovered just how flexible she needed to be when the goats arrived late in the rehearsal period and suddenly all the blocking had to be changed. Also, goats being famously recalcitrant, there were times when Pepsi arbitrarily refused to be dragged in on her leash and Emily had to carry her (she weighed 25 to 40 pounds). But she and Domingo developed a whole range of silent communication involving the goat. "It added another layer to our relationship," said Domingo. "Some days we'd be in love with each other and some days we'd be frustrated because of the goat. Emily would sometimes come over and snatch the goat from me. Little dynamics like that would change depending on whether the goat was cooperative." He added, "You have to go with what's happening onstage and make a moment out of it. Don't start your monologue when the animal's acting up. Let it happen and support it." When the goat started nibbling the trees, he learned to acknowledge it. Similarly, when the dog in *Two Gentlemen* growled at him, he had to go with it. I can't think of a better lesson in listening, allowing, and being here now.

Lesson #8: Make sure the animal is neither stressed nor mistreated.

Is this your personal responsibility? Maybe not, but it's the right thing to do.

Bill Berloni told me that a few years ago in *Don Giovanni* at the Met, some people in the company discovered the horses, rented for a show from a local stable, were being tranquilized. The company members called the *New York Times,* who investigated (and called Berloni, who also works for the Humane Society). "Some actors, because they want to work for that theatre again, don't want to be the whistle blower," said Berloni. "But SAG now has a clause in which an actor can refuse to do a particular scene, with no ramifications. Actors can call up their SAG representative and say, 'I don't want to work with that animal because of the way it's handled.'"

Actors can also call their local humane societies to report abuse, or they can call the American Humane Association in Los Angeles, the film watchdog group that provides guidelines for proper treatment of animals who act. The Association will investigate and intervene if necessary. Stage and film actors are encouraged to call with their concerns or simply for advice on how to work with their animals. The number is (818) 501-0123 (website: www.ahafilm.org).

Lesson #9: Enjoy the opportunity.

"What is so appealing about an animal onstage is that we're not seeing acting, we're seeing honesty," said Berloni. "The ultimate actor is looking for truth but still fabricating it. But the animal is all about truth, which is why we're so drawn to it." He added, "The level of audience interest increases when an animal walks onstage. If you're the actor fortunate enough to be in that scene, people will remember you and what you've done with that animal. But if you're insincere and act like you don't care, the audience will hate you. It takes them out of the play." He concluded, "When an animal's onstage, it's an exciting moment in live theatre."

Chapter 15

MUSICAL INSTRUMENTS

Audiences are always delighted when an actor proves to be more than a one-trick pony. They're especially enchanted when a performer can act, sing, dance . . . and play a musical instrument. Or two. How do these quadruple-threat wunderkinds integrate their musicianship with their acting skills?

The actors I talked to—two pianists, a guitarist, and a violist/violinist—were musicians before they were actors, except for concert pianist/composer Hershey Felder, who started both simultaneously. All four have been playing instruments for most of their lives.

First, a word about casting: If you play an instrument, you've got a leg up in the business. Accomplished musician/actors are rare enough that Dennis Jones, director of a California regional theatre production of *Pump Boys & Dinettes*, had to go to New York to find an actor/pianist, John C. Brown. Jones also had to cancel a planned production of *Swingtime Canteen* when he couldn't find enough women for the all-female band.

JV Mercanti was casting associate at the Roundabout Theatre in New York, where *Cabaret* originated before going on to tour the country. When I talked to him during the national tour, he said casting replacements was an ongoing challenge. Auditioners were judged as musicians first, but ultimately, said Mercanti, "They've got to be a killer in every category," which includeded song and dance. (They also had to look right for Weimar-era Germany.)

Of course, getting a good role is never a shoo-in. In the touring company of *Cabaret,* Shana Mahoney, who played both viola (her first instrument) and violin as a member of the Kit Kat Club Band, went through five grueling auditions. "In between callbacks I'd take lessons, dragging my instruments on the subway," she said. She noted that among the show's cast at the time were a couple of "core musicians," but most were actors proficient with instruments, having played their whole lives off and on. A few, though, dug out their instruments and dusted them off for the audition. "A stringed instrument," she noted, "is harder to pick up just for a show; it requires more consistent discipline."

So what exactly is the mental process that actors use to segue organically from dialogue to instrument playing and back again?

"It's almost like having to learn two shows," said John C. Brown. "The music needs its own separate rehearsal process in my brain until I get comfortable enough to just play it." Before rehearsals commenced, he familiarized himself with the *Pump Boys* album. Once rehearsals started, he created personal connections for himself in his role as L.M., the "sexy, bookish one." He envisioned his piano as a rolltop desk, with little index cards for his chord symbols (in *Pump Boys* only the chords are set) because the sheet music book was too large and cumbersome. He also had a picture of Dolly Parton on his desk/piano, because he sang a song about her.

To make the transition from dialogue to piano playing, he devised an intention, and he listened and allowed just the way he'd do in a straight role. "If somebody else is singing, I just become the band," he said. "If I'm singing [while playing], it's the same as though I'm doing a monologue. I focus on the other actors and let them dictate the piano solo through my hands, just the way you'd deliver a line differently every night depending on how another actor is delivering lines to you."

Brown, who also played piano as Chico Marx in the stage version of *Animal Crackers*, said there's a fine line you can find yourself bouncing back and forth across when rehearsing: "John C. Brown thinking about the notes you're playing versus Chico Marx just *doing* it." If you're not in character as you start to play, suddenly "it becomes about the piano"—which, of course, you don't want. "When you're onstage as an actor with an instrument, it's not about technically executing the song correctly," he elaborated. "You do it just like you would as an actor—you look the other actor in the eye and tell the truth." In the case of *Pump Boys*, Brown conducted wordless dialogues with the other actor/musicians while playing: "We'd listen and look and play off each other as actors would, except our hands are our instruments."

And when he did something onstage that he hadn't practiced, he'd try to repeat the "mistake" so the audience wouldn't know. "That helps me to stay in character rather than think, Oh damn, I screwed that up. And we share looks with other musicians when someone botches something. It's fun to share that with band. It makes the show more exciting, new and fresh."

Hershey Felder, who talked to me when he was appearing in his original solo play with music, *George Gershwin Alone*, in Los Angeles, said that he imagines scenes from Gershwin's life when performing, to identify with how Gershwin (who died in 1937) might have felt as he composed and played.

"Suddenly it's like his ghost appears to me. Not that I'm bringing his ghost to life, but I start to feel, My God, there was a real life there. I'm doing exactly what he did, touching the same notes, feeling the same things." He noted, "Playing the piano as an actor, you can't let go of yourself too much, though, or you'll lose it—you have to maintain technique."

Felder of course is playing a real-life character who was in fact a pianist, so the sheer musicianship is important.

For *Cabaret*'s Shana Mahoney, the task was somewhat different. She created a detailed backstory for her character, which she said was quite helpful and tended to evolve as the show continued. "I think of my character as coming from the countryside of Austria," she explained. "She studied violin and viola her whole life and left home for Berlin, lying to her parents and telling them she's working at the Berlin Symphony Orchestra." Her character's objective, she said, is to simply get through the night doing her job. Given circumstances: She's exhausted from having done eight shows already that night but needs the money. "Sometimes there are nights when I feel like that!" she laughed.

When guitarist Scott Waara appeared in *The People versus Mona* at Pasadena Playhouse, he entered into an onstage world where everybody played instruments, in fact several apiece. Waara himself played percussion as well as electric, acoustic, and slide guitar. "It was a conceit of the show," he said. "You forget about the fact that you play. It's just another action." In South Coast Rep's *The Education of Randy Newman*, he played only one guitar piece, at the end of the first act.

I asked him how he went about playing the guitar not as Scott Waara but as his character, whom he describes as "Randy Newman–like." (The real Newman, of course, plays piano, not guitar.) "Any guy that stands up and plays an instrument is expressing an extension of himself," said Waara, who's performed often with bands. "So in the context of this play I'm also expressing an extension of myself as this character. It's no different from any other kind of acting. You just happen to be playing a guitar at the moment."

Shana Mahoney pinpointed a difference in her style when playing her instruments in character in *Cabaret*. "I put the viola between my legs, wrap my arms around it seductively," she said. "When we play in the entr'acte, I'm stomping my feet, jumping up and down, spinning my instrument. Technically, though, it's how I really play it, but maybe just a little bouncier."

As for Felder, he said his own approach to the piano is traditional and classical. To play as Gershwin, he had to teach himself to be snappier. "The result is I'm not as self-indulgent," he observed. He also noted that he found it easier to accept applause in character as Gershwin rather than in his own rather shy persona. However, he emphasized that he didn't try to imitate Gershwin but rather to interpret him, to present Gershwin's passion for music through Hershey Felder's own sensibilities.

What about the technical challenges that can arise when you add instrument playing into an already demanding theatrical mix? Waara said *The People versus Mona* presented some obstacles. "No one's counting you in, no one's holding you together. In an ordinary band you can turn around, signal each other, someone is kind of leading, calling tunes, changes, and tempos. Whereas if you're in a play, telling a story, everything's tightly scripted and you can't have any extraneous movement." There was also a learning curve; some of the cast members were musicians only, others were actor/musicians. Some actually learned an instrument for the play (although they all had some musical background). During rehearsal, people would jokingly yell for *chord* instead of *line*.

Ultimately, said Waara, "you can't be thinking about your playing. I think a great musician is thinking not about his playing but about what he's trying to communicate. You can't be thinking about where your hands are going. But that's the same as any prop—when you're pouring coffee onstage, you're not thinking about the coffee."

The catch is that you don't have to train and practice to pour coffee. Mahoney showed up every night at 5:45 to rosin her bows, tune both instruments, and warm up her fingers before going on to physical and vocal warm-ups. She also practiced at least fifteen minutes a day. Before that, she'd practice only "once in a blue moon." Waara ran scales every night for *Mona*. "Playing an instrument adds to the tension," he conceded. "I'd come home and start practicing for another hour and a half during the rehearsal period. Once you get it in your fingers, you can begin to loosen up a little bit."

Does the acting suffer when you're concentrating so hard on your playing? "It might have arced a little later than it would have otherwise," said Waara. "But it was worth it."

Indeed, all agreed that playing an instrument while acting is terrifically fun and challenging. By the end of a year on tour, Mahoney was looking forward to playing her instruments more than to the dancing and singing. She hypothesized that was because she was growing more artistically from playing and practicing so much, "whereas with singing and dancing I'm already at a certain level." She added, "It's so gratifying, artistically, to have so many things to focus on. You never get bored."

Musing on his role as Gershwin, Hershey Felder summed it up: "Music is the expression after you've finished making your point in dialogue. It's an explosion of the feeling." How do you make it happen? "You work and work, you get every affectation out of the way, and just tell the truth. The audience doesn't want to see you 'performing.'"

Chapter 16

MONOLOGUES

We usually think of the monologue as either an audition piece or as a solo performance. But let's discuss the fine points of doing a monologue within a play. A long hunk of text, usually extra specially intense and deeply revealing of the character, a monologue is spoken either 1) directly to the audience, 2) to another or others onstage, or 3) ostensibly to oneself (a soliloquy).

You'd think there would be three separate sets of rules for those three different types of monologues, but no, there's only one overriding rule: Don't think of it as a monologue; think of it as a dialogue. That applies across the board. (For techniques on memorizing the monologue, see Chapter 27, "Memorization.")

Let's say you're talking to a silent onstage actor. How that actor responds to you should affect your delivery—whether he or she frowns at you, raises a disbelieving eyebrow, seems about to interrupt you, smiles encouragingly, etc. The audience can take the place of the silent onstage actor; if you can't actually see them over the footlights, you can sense their reactions.

But what if you're alone onstage and the fourth wall is intact? It's easy to justify talking to yourself. In *A Challenge for the Actor,* Hagen lists many reasons why someone might do so in real life, including to pull yourself together, remember a piece of information, out of frustration, just to amuse yourself, to solve a problem.

But even then, you can think of it as a dialogue rather than as talking to yourself. The great classical actor Morris Carnovsky, in performing Shakespeare's soliloquies, objectified himself so that he perceived himself as talking to an alter ego, an extroverted self. "The character," he wrote, "in a certain sense, is talking to a partner in his thinking. Another person is involved, even though that other person is himself, the projection of himself."

Actor Jason Butler Harner thinks there's always *someone* to talk to—even if it's the gods.

I called Harner because I saw him in a memorable production of *Long Day's Journey into Night* at American Conservatory Theater. There's a one-and-a-half-page monologue (which can seem much longer than that) that Edmund delivers to his father ("When I was on the square-head square-rigger bound for Buenos Aires," he intones). I was impressed with the way Harner as Edmund handled that lyrical, potentially snore-inducing speech, and I wanted to find out how he pulled it off.

The first step was trying to get his mind around what he was saying, because it was so ethereal. "I tried to figure out when he was being honest and saying something directly active, and when he was shying away from revealing his vulnerability, for instance. I spent a lot of time looking at everything he quotes, thinking about what those quotes meant and why he would bring them up at a certain time."

In the more poetic passages, said Harner, he spent a lot of time with each word, immersing himself in whatever images they conjured up for him personally. "I'd think of a phrase like 'square-head square rigger' and what it meant." Harner mentioned an exercise called "Cave of the Word," where you work your way slowly through a poem, exploring each and every sound, letting it resonate sensorially, letting it prompt impulsive articulation and movement. "I'd think about the 's' sounds of 'square-head square rigger,' I would wonder why they were placed together that way.

"I spent some time thinking about each image, what it meant to be feeling alone at the top of this ship and tell that as frankly as possible," he continued. "That work happens in its own time—getting to a place where you create a memory not from your own life."

He also took a few field trips—a ferry boat ride, a climb onto a cliff over the beach—to help visualize some of the images, but ultimately never settled on an image of the boat itself.

But here's the important thing: "I didn't ever want to work too hard on getting the audience to understand the images," he said. "What will anchor you is your action, what's at stake. When I made that decision—that this monologue is about inviting my father into my life for the first time, or however I phrased the action that night—that helped anchor me."

Harner and I discussed the ways that monologues often go astray. "[Sometimes] they sound pretty but don't really move the story forward," he said. "I set a goal for myself that if I was going to err, it would be on the side of being too small and off the cuff rather than too pretty or romantic." He added, "I think that an audience understands where a character like Edmund is in that moment much better if he's just being and relating as opposed to articulating and demonstrating."

He also pointed out that actors sometimes get so worried about the pacing that they race through the monologue. He advised deliberately taking too much time in rehearsal so you get a better sense of what you really need. "Sometimes you think, I need to keep moving, keep entertaining—but an audience may need you to sit there for a second so they can connect. That's scary though. It's hard to tell when an actor is allowing that moment or creating it and manipulating the audience."

Sometimes, too, said Harner, you get so involved in making your speech be the cornerstone of the character, The Moment, that it stands apart and changes the line or rhythm of the play. Or else it passes by so fast that neither you nor the audience really absorb it.

How do you launch into a long monologue like Edmund's? "I never wanted it to smell like 'This is the monologue,' so I tried to slide into it as gracefully as possible, not 'announcing' it," Harner said. This was a challenge, because O'Neill has Edmund blatantly declare, "You've just told me some of your memories, here are some highlights of mine." Harner slithered past those lines subtly indeed, as I recall. Maybe that's connected to the fact that he pored over the text to figure out what lines he could virtually throw away in order to gain something else.

"If I had had to attack that monologue six years ago," he mused, "it would have been 'This happened, then this, then *this* happened.'" It's important to know what the operative words are, but, said Harner, "there's a higher state where you know what the operative word is, but is there another way of phrasing it that illuminates it in a different way?"

The key, though, is that he played off Josef Sommer, the distinguished actor in the role of James Tyrone. Although by opening night Harner had a personalized understanding of Edmund's relationship with his father, and had settled on overall objectives in relation to him, his nightly delivery of that monologue (and of course his entire performance) differed depending on how he felt and what he was getting back from Sommer. "Sometimes that monologue was generous and tearful, a gift to my father," explained Harner. "Sometimes it was self-deprecating and jokey. There were even moments when it was an attack on my father . . . And there were moments I was particularly emotionally connected to every night. When Edmund says, 'It was a great mistake being born a man, I would have been more successful as a seagull or a fish,' I knew that was always there. So I could use it to be generous and get my father to understand me, or I could be self-deprecating and let him do the work." How Sommer related his own preceding story, whether Harner felt the two characters were getting along, whether he felt his father was seeing who he was at that moment—all that affected his delivery on any given night.

Harner's solid homework, his focus on his objective, and his ability to let all that go and truly listen and respond in the moment, paid off: His—well, let's call it an unmonologue—was riveting. Here are some practical hints:

- Keep your subtext rich. Your mind should always be full of thoughts.

- Don't place an imaginary person anywhere specific; instead see him or her in your mind's eye. To get a feeling for how you would do this naturally, observe yourself the next time you find that you're vacuuming the living room rug while rehashing a fight you just had with someone, saying the things you wish you'd been clever enough to say at the time. Where are your eyes looking? Nowhere.

- Similarly, if alone onstage, don't play it as though it were really happening, complete with realistic gestures. Hagen points out that when you're alone, your body and voice don't behave the same way they do in public. For example, when alone, you might be unpacking the groceries as you mutter angrily to an imaginary director. She also notes that you'd never enter a room for the sole purpose of babbling to yourself; you'd be doing something specific, then you'd find yourself talking out loud.

- In fact, don't use too many gestures at all, cautioned Stella Adler in *The Technique of Acting.* Harner noted that actors tend to want to use their hands or their voice to create images that the audience can visualize. Resist the impulse. Simplify. "What happens when you *don't* use hand gestures?" Harner challenged.

- If your (non)monologue is about a problem, find the solution *in real time, as you go* (Hagen).

Acting teacher Jean Shelton summed it up for me: "Stay within the situation. Have an objective. Don't drop out to create your imagery onstage; do your image work in advance and then let it go." Gotcha.

Chapter 17

CHILDREN

The children and adolescents I've seen onstage, most of them profession-ally trained and experienced, have ranged from pretty good (stage presence, confident delivery, but a tendency to be cute or to not really listen) to flat-out great. And in films and on TV, we've seen kids like Haley Joel Osment to name a prominent example, who've knocked our socks off. Overall, whatever skill level the youngsters have achieved, I've noticed that the relationships between the adult actors and the kids seemed solid. How do adult actors forge that all-important bond with a child or teenager? And what special precautions do we old fogies need to take, if any, when working with kids?

For starters, you only have them five hours a day, so you have to work hard. Linda Hoy, a TV and stage veteran who has also taught children's theatre, has worked often with kids. "Kids are learning how to behave, the proper etiquette and procedure," said Hoy. As an example, she noted that whereas an adult who goofed onstage would presumably acknowledge it and go on, one of the young actors she was working with was reluctant to cop to it when he made a mistake.

"We're all tired," said Hoy, "but kids don't know how to pull on that extra reserve of energy." In a show she was in, one exhausted kid's diction got sloppy, he yawned onstage, his eyes would wander. She buoyed him up by picking up her cues, keeping her speeches tight, and resolutely maintaining eye contact. "I was much more focused with him," she said. "Working with kids you learn patience and focus. It's a different kind of energy with children."

Or kids can tend to go automatically from cue to line to cue, getting the comic timing down right but not really engaging with their co-actor. Often that's because they've been encouraged to be funny and play a "quality" rather than really listening and allowing. Craig Slaight, director of American Conservatory Theater's Young Conservatory, told me that sometimes youngsters arrive there with previous training that needs to be "deconstructed."

Hoy tries to be as upbeat as possible throughout rehearsal and performance, giving lots of positive feedback. She feels that negativity of any kind can be damaging around kids. On the plus side, she observed that in one cast, "The kids had their lines before we did. Young minds!"

Another actor mentioned that some kids are shy, others more relaxed around adult actors. He spent extra time hanging out with his shy co-star in *A Thousand Clowns* until the boy felt comfortable with him.

Are the rules different when you're working onscreen? Hoy believes that films can ruin children for theatre; they don't learn how to sustain a performance. In theatre, she said, it's easier for them; they can create a whole world and live in that world. "In film the mistakes are gone away. You don't learn how to build a continuum. In film, they live in sound bites."

I remember a particularly brilliant film performance, though, by then-Thirteen-year-old Kimberly J. Brown in *Tumbleweeds*. Kimberly, who has worked professionally since the age of five, including in an Emmy-nominated role on TV's *The Guiding Light,* played the daughter of a working-class single mom. The rapport between the two was palpable. I asked her onscreen mother, Janet McTeer, how she and Kimberly achieved that closeness.

"Kimberly knew what she was doing, knew how adults would treat her, and so I decided that shouldn't be the case," said McTeer, a Brit who trained at the Royal Academy of Dramatic Art, was nominated for an Oscar for *Tumbleweeds,* and is also a Tony Award–winner (for Nora in *A Doll's House*). "I felt she shouldn't know what she was in, it should be a completely new creative venture. So whenever I felt she was doing something that she recognized, I'd try and do something different. And we had a ball."

During the week-long rehearsal, the cast did a lot of improvisations. When Kimberly got stuck in line readings, said McTeer, "we would josh her out of it until it had the kind of really easy quality that the whole thing needed. When she lost focus, I would give her completely the wrong line." Can you do that onstage, too? I wondered. "Absolutely," said McTeer. "I've done it with the kids onstage in *A Doll's House.* They're kids—you have to keep them alive."

McTeer was always honest with Kimberly, and didn't hesitate to say things like, "Kimberly, I'm having a hard time with this scene, could you not fuck about quite so much in the corner?" or "Kimberly, stop, go away and play, I'm having to work too hard." At the same time she also treated Kimberly like a peer. "I'd say to her, 'Oh, God, why am I finding this scene so hard?' I'd talk to her like I'd talk to another actor."

Along the lines of treating children like peers, Craig Slaight recommends playing a mentorship role. "Adult actors don't appear to children as authority figures, the way directors do," he said. They feel more like partners. That gives the actor an opportunity to offer advice to the child that he or she might absorb more easily than if it came from a director. Of course, you don't want to offer them a belligerent "Don't do that!" Benign criticism is what's needed. You should definitely not assume that kids know everything and that they're feeling comfortable, Slaight noted, even if they're acting cocky. It's helpful to explain things to them, even such seemingly obvious things as, "You know, when the director is talking to us, it really helps to listen, because we might need to know these things later."

There's no reason to hesitate to play a mentorship role. Probably all actors who are young or new to the trade could use a mentor. Young Jillian Wheeler, who by the age of ten had been in movies, soaps, commercials, and musicals, profited enormously from working onstage in regional theatre with Lynn Redgrave, who coached her on a British accent, and Holly Hunter. Both women took Jillian under their wings. "Holly taught her a lot about discipline, because it was such an intense role," said Jillian's mother, Mary Wheeler. Lynn Redgrave, she said, was "incredibly gracious." Similarly, twelve-year-old pro Hayden Panettierre enjoyed a great relationship with Calista Flockhart when she played the thin one's daughter in *Ally McBeal*. And in the TV show *One on One*, teenaged Kyla Pratt told me she learned a lot from Flex Alexander, who played her dad: "He teaches us how to stay grounded, when it's time to work and time to play."

There's a caveat here, though, warned Slaight. You should safeguard the young person's privacy. No matter how kids are behaving, they're probably extremely vulnerable and very easily embarrassed in public. They don't want to be singled out as the know-nothing, and they can easily get defensive. So take your little colleague aside when offering advice, such as—if they're not listening—"You know, it really helps me when you look at me when you do that."

When you can be a mentor and establish a good relationship, the experience can be very satisfying for all concerned. Working with pros makes kids want to reach, to challenge themselves, said Linda Hoy. "They're able to go deeper if asked to go deeper," concurred Slaight, who has directed everyone "from Julie Harris to eight-year-olds." "If they're treated as peers, they're so empowered by being asked to rise to the occasion that they're unflaggingly resilient." Plus, he said, there's often a fresher imagination at work among children, a sense of wonderment that we adults lose as we get more jaded.

Working with kids may take extra energy and patience, but there can be rewards too. Hoy reported that her kids were affectionate and fun backstage. As for young Kimberly, Janet McTeer said, months after the shoot, "We're still really good friends. Madly in love."

Chapter 18

X-TREME MAKEUP

If your stage or screen makeup is so heavy that it takes hours to apply and utterly transforms you, who is calling the shots, you or the makeup?

Laurence Olivier wouldn't have batted a (false) eyelash over the problem. He was known for his insistence upon theatrical makeup. Nowadays, the big prosthetic nose he favored for his Shylock wouldn't be acceptable, of course. Nevertheless, the way he fit his makeup to his character—and vice versa—is an important part of the actor's craft.

Three professionals who have worked under such extreme conditions agreed that the fit goes both ways.

Armin Shimerman (who played Quark in the cast of the TV *Star Trek* series *Deep Space Nine* during the entire seven years of its run) and Andrew Robinson (who appeared in the recurring role of Garak in the same series) are classically trained actors who say that performing under heavy makeup is similar to mask work. The paradox is that as restrictive as masks (or gobs of makeup) can be, they also have the capacity to free you emotionally.

"The classical reference I would use is commedia dell'arte," said Robinson, whose granddaughter nervously refused to look at him in his *Deep Space* face. "Like a mask, the heavy makeup 'sets' your face." As the fearsome humanoid Garak, he wore seven prosthetic pieces plus heavy cosmetics, which initially took three-and-a-half to four hours to apply (but eventually narrowed down to two hours). Tall and imposing-looking on the small screen, Robinson had weird ridges on his face that looked like motionless serpents under the skin, and a scaly reptilian neck. He initially felt claustrophobic, as though his face were being squeezed and he couldn't breathe, but "Once I got over that there was a real freedom. I could support bigger gestures, greater vocal power, my eyes could function in a more stylistic way. Obviously I was restricted by the seven pieces glued on me so that me, Andy, was submerged. But out of that, this character came together."

He did Indian kathakali eye exercises for strengthening purposes, because with restricted facial movement, all his expression had to register in his eyes, voice, and body. "The stronger the eyes are, the more information you're able to convey," he said. "Without the 'mask' that kind of eyework would be overacting [on TV]." His voice became deeper, more deliberate. "I tried to extract the value of each word, each phrase. A lot of the choices I made were external choices. The sci fi genre is not naturalism. So there's a great deal of freedom to search for alien behavior. How does an alien speak?" He thinks of that show as a combination of commedia and restoration drama: "It required that kind of style. So the actors that were the most successful with the mask are those who are theatre trained, especially classical."

I asked him what were the pitfalls of working with heavy makeup. "What happens with a lot of actors is the 'mask' gets thrown on them, and they become intimidated by it," he said. "If you're doing Greek tragedy in a traditional way, you learn how to work with these elements, which were designed to elevate the performance above naturalism. . . . You can't slouch and mumble like on *Melrose Place*."

Armin Shimerman—Robinson's friend, *Deep Space Nine* colleague, and associate at Los Angeles' Matrix Theatre—disagreed with Robinson's commedia comparison: "Commedia is a very large performance, very demonstrative," he said. "My feeling about the 'mask' is it still must be very real yet theatrical. It's like performing on a large stage and having to convey emotions through the eyes and experiences, but not necessarily overact." He added, "You wouldn't say Olivier was an *over*actor—just a *large* actor."

Shimerman's Quark, a crafty little bugger of the Ferengi species, was less human-looking than Robinson's intimidating Garak. Shimerman's entire head was surrounded by a rubber football-helmet affair, put on with medical adhesive, with a mask attached to it; only his chin and part of his throat remained uncovered. The result was an oversized, bulbous, bifurcated bald noggin that resembled a lumpy butt. He had ridges on his forehead, which wrapped around to connect to Dumbo-like ears. His nose was broad and ridged, and he had pointy, widely spaced teeth. (Why are aliens always so darned ugly?) Although the makeup felt at first as distracting, said Shimerman, as a fly buzzing around your head, such is the *Star Trek* series artistry that it was actually quite malleable. Over the course of nine years (including the follow-up, *The Next Generation*), the makeup went from four down to two hours to apply.

How did his complicated Ferengi-head affect Shimerman's approach to the role? Describing himself as normally a "circumspect" actor, he said, "It was a bit claustrophobic the first time. I thought it would be repressive, would cut off my actor impulses because I couldn't hear as well. On the other hand, it was freeing, like wearing a paper bag over your face at a party. It's not you.

Most actors worry about what they look like on camera, but to me it made no difference; I could do whatever I wanted to do."

He noted that the casting department on that series tended to hire classical actors who are used to being larger than life. "The makeup does tone down your reactions and you have to bump things up, like on the stage. Once I realized I couldn't overact, it was very freeing. It inspired me." His sly Quark was in fact both comic and subtle.

Shimerman believes the major danger for actors is in overcompensating. "Actors see the makeup and they think they have to make faces," he said. "But you're in makeup, the audience sees it, you don't have to overenhance it. If you're a one-legged man, you don't have to *play* a one-legged man, you are what you are. Many actors tend to come up with buffoonish performances."

He added, "Andy feels you have to fill the makeup, but I think he'd agree with me: not too much. I'd say you don't have to fill the makeup, but you have to do *something*. But not doing anything seems to me the lesser fault."

Shimerman became a more daring and fantastical actor because of that makeup. "I learned to play the fool. I'm not sure whether it was the makeup or the character himself, but in my mind those two are intertwined. I learned to be much more open."

On stage, of course, overly made up or not, you're expected to be bigger than on camera. In *Ugly's First World* by Jeff Dorchen, a 1999 production at Los Angeles' Actors' Gang, Christopher Gerson and two others played zombies. Gerson's makeup was made of layers of latex and tissue paper; he pulled at it after it was applied to break it open slightly so that it looked even more repulsive. He also had a slit in his neck, one ear taped to his head and latexed over, and blacked-out teeth, and he shaved his head and stained it with charcoal. Every night, makeup took one and a half hours, and required isopropyl mirastate to dissolve the latex afterward. "It would have been difficult to do it every night if it hadn't been something I liked," said Gerson.

Not only did he like the role, he discovered his character through the makeup. And not a minute too soon: He got his makeup for the first time two days before tech week. "It was as if [prior to that] I had created a character who was just a base coat, and then I suddenly painted the thing," he explained. When he first looked in the mirror, he thought, "My goodness, he's in bad shape! No wonder he's not a positive person! It's a bit simplistic, but it does make you understand the depth of your character." He saw that his eyes remained clear within the gory makeup, and he realized that even though his character was a walking horror, he was still intelligent. Because the whites of his eyes popped out so noticeably from his black and blood-red face, he and the director decided he'd keep his head low most of the time and save those startling whites for special moments.

In masks or makeup, the eyes definitely have it: Shimerman's and Robinson's intensely animated, light-colored eyes were riveting in the three episodes I watched.

"It's a huge mistake not to let the makeup bring something out in you," Gerson said. "It can take you to the wrong place, but it's the director's job to take you to the right area. It has to transform you in some way."

All three actors benefited hugely from the daily grueling makeup sessions. Robinson said he went into a sort of trance during the makeup sessions. "For most actors it's frustrating to sit in a chair for hours having someone apply cold glue to the face," said Shimerman, "but the upside is it gives you time to get ready for work." He ran lines with others, got into character, worked on the language. "Mondays my call would be at 4 or 5 a.m.," he said. "Andy and I had fourteen- to sixteen-hour days normally." Taking the makeup off, of course, is less rewarding after a long day or exhausting performance, and it has to be removed slowly to avoid damaging the skin. For Robinson, it took the better part of an hour. Gerson often drove home without bothering to remove his zombie face, occasionally eliciting a scream from passing motorists.

Clearly, outlandish makeup calls for a certain amount of working from the outside in to create your character. And why not? Our own personalities are at least partly formed by our physical appearance. But where our natural faces may limit us in real life, in acting our artificial faces can free us.

Chapter 19

CIGARETTES

We've come a long way, baby, since Bogie looked sexy with a cigarette dangling from his lip. Because American attitudes have changed so drastically, smoking on stage and screen has become an issue. Smoking—the final frontier.

Stage director Tom Ross first encountered the problem when directing the British play *Abigail's Party* by Mike Leigh. Like all Leigh's scripts, it calls for excessive smoking. Leigh develops his material improvisationally with his actors; presumably, European-style, they smoke like chimneys.

The house was exceptionally tiny—about sixty-five seats—so Ross cut out all references to smoking in the script. Ironically, local critics familiar with Leigh's work called attention to the glaring absence thereof.

Then Ross directed *The Homecoming*. "I thought, oh my God, I can't cut cigarettes out of the sacred Pinter text," he said. "*Abigail's Party* was slice of life. But in Pinter people use cigarettes as power ploys, offering them to one another."

Luckily he discovered magic-trick cigarettes. Expensive, and bought in magic shops, they are actually plastic tubes that you blow into rather than suck. There's a little piece of red tinfoil at the end where the ember would be, which picks up theatrical light well, and when you blow into the tube, it emits a powder that resembles smoke.

That worked so well that Ross also used the trick cigs in Irish playwright Conor McPherson's *The Weir*. Because it is set in an Irish pub, it would have been quite peculiar had no one lit up. Ross stocked ashtrays with real cigarette butts, and the actors took a few tokes of the phony fags, then casually placed them in the ashtray. I saw both *The Weir* and *The Homecoming*, and was mystified that I couldn't smell smoke, even though I was close enough to touch the actors—the faux cigarettes were that believable.

In fact, at a performance of *The Weir*, when one of the actors made a curtain speech to solicit donations for AIDS, an audience member yelled at him about the dangers of second-hand smoke. When he explained, she threatened to cancel her season subscription anyway because the theatre was glamorizing smoking.

"Never mind that we're all drinking, like, twelve drinks and then driving away in a car [in the play]!" laughed cast member Emily Ackerman, who took it as a compliment when audience members start coughing and waving their programs around, which they inevitably did. Ackerman, who smokes occasionally, was at first uncomfortable with the fake cigarettes, wishing they were real. But she and the others worked to make them seem natural, and to avoid things like too much "smoke" shooting out the end. "I tried to 'inhale' and 'exhale' when the audience focus was elsewhere," she said. Trick cigarettes mean one more technical thing to deal with. But it's an important part of the play; when a pub regular offered newcomer Ackerman a cigarette, she had to accept it, "so that says something. If you cut [smoking] out, you're cutting out text and character information."

The fact is that if you're doing a period piece—say, Noel Coward—or a contemporary play set outside North America, you're doing a disservice to the playwright to eliminate such an important and often revealing social custom. When Northern Ireland playwright Gary Mitchell's drama *Trust* premiered in San Francisco, Mitchell, who came out for rehearsals and opening, was amazed to discover that Californians don't smoke. In Belfast and elsewhere in Europe, there's a whole etiquette and ritual to smoking, which Mitchell had incorporated into the play: Everyone offers cigarettes to everyone. If you get up to go to the bathroom and someone brings out a pack while you're gone, there will be a cigarette at your place when you return. So in *Trust*, if one person smoked, everyone had to, and the cigarettes were real.

Dan Hiatt, the only *Trust* cast member who didn't smoke in real life at the time, said that production did get him going again for a few months. "The thing I hate about onstage smoking is that actors only smoke about a half-inch and put it out because there's no time," he commented. "It seems unreal. In *Trust*, we pretty much finished off our cigarettes." A big, quiet fan had been installed over the stage, connected to a duct, and no audience member complained. Wealthier operations, like Broadway houses, have fancier fan systems.

Hiatt recalled an outdoor production of *Hamlet* he'd been in, a modern adaptation in which Rosencrantz and Guildenstern smoked. "The minute they'd light up, even with a thirty-mile wind blowing, people started coughing," he said.

Once, watching a production of Mike Leigh's *Ecstasy*, I imagined I had a sore throat by the end, with the five working-class Brits onstage virtually chain-smoking. In that case, the cast smoked nicotine-free herbal cigarettes (put into Silk Cut packets), which tend to smell marijuana-like. They also burn more quickly, enabling the actors in this play to stick to the stage directions, which required much lighting up. Beth Donohue, who played Dawn and was smoking lightly in real life at the time, said she actually only took two or three puffs per cig, then put it out. With all the smoking going on, I certainly didn't notice. One of the actors had recently quit smoking and was chewing nicotine gum at the time. Being in the play didn't lure him back to the evil weed.

As in *Trust*, the ritual of smoking in *Ecstasy* had social implications, with everyone offering everyone else cigarettes, and insisting, "Oh, no, smoke mine!" even when they were both smoking the same brand.

Donohue said she's gone through long nonsmoking periods during which she's been in shows where she had to smoke but was able to resist the pull to start up again. However, she knows actors who have recently quit smoking and who would therefore turn down smoking roles—at least for the time being. "Smoking is a powerful thing onstage sensorially," she said. "I don't think you can do it lightly. A little bit goes a long way." If she's smoking in real life at the time, she usually smokes at least one cigarette before curtain, because "I don't want to introduce something shocking to my system onstage. That way, I won't get a rush or shaky hands." For playing Dawn, she went through the script and marked every point where Dawn lit up. "It was always directly related to a conflict she was trying to avoid, or an emotion she was trying not to feel," said Donohue. "You can funnel your emotions into a cigarette. For me, it was an important aspect of her character rather than a style choice."

What about smoking onscreen, where the distractions of audience members fanning, coughing, and kvetching are not an issue? The actor, whether a nonsmoker, a smoker, or an ex-smoker, still has to cope with the problem of inhaling those coffin nails in just the right way—and presumably on screen the trick cigarettes won't do.

Long-reformed smoker William B. Davis had to smoke regularly during his seven seasons on *The X-Files* as the nameless "smoking man." "I was perceived by Mulder et al. as the epitome of evil," explained Davis. "So smoking showed my character's complete disregard of law, his complete arrogance—he'll smoke anywhere—his disregard for his own health, and it says something about his psychological state of mind. On a metaphorical level, because he represents the devil, smoking suggests fire. It was all quite integral to his character and his place in the storyline." Davis held the cigarette distinctively between thumb and first or second finger; one director said that the cigarette to the character was like sex.

Davis used real cigarettes on the first few episodes—and yes, he inhaled—before deciding that wasn't such a good idea for an ex-smoker. He then switched to herbal cigarettes, which not only burn more quickly but also more steadily, and light more easily—although they create more ash, necessitating constant brushing-down by the wardrobe people.

The technical aspects of smoking on screen, said Davis, can be tricky. "Suppose we shoot a master shot," he explained, "and decide I've been smoking before the scene starts, so we start with a three-quarter-length cigarette. Each time we do a new take on the master shot, we have to light a new three-quarter-length cigarette. Then when we go into coverage, we have to match the length of the cigarette to the master shot. So for any given scene one might smoke thirty to forty cigarettes, and each time they had to be lit." Most of his actual drags were taken in between shots as he lit the cigarette.

Fortunately he discovered a gizmo that lights cigarettes mechanically, and from that point on, the props people lit his cigarettes and handed them to him for each take. "In truth there wasn't as much smoking as you would think," he said.

Nevertheless, what there was had to be carefully handled. "While in the master, one might cavalierly smoke whenever one felt the urge, after that one has to smoke at exactly the same time, using the same hand, the exact same length of puffs. Another complication was that the cigarette was part of the design of the shot usually, so they wanted the smoke in a certain relationship to the light, the cigarette held a certain number of millimeters in relation to your nose."

Despite the technical considerations, said Davis, it's nice to an actor to have something physical to ground your sense of reality. "It helped me," he said, "and as an ex-smoker it felt natural and easy. Arrogance and smoking seem to connect well for me. The activity of smoking would connect me immediately to the whole feel of the character, the backstory. Even when I did a scene that didn't involve smoking, often prior to the take I'd mime smoking, and that physical rhythm would put me into the emotional space of the character."

The only complaint Davis ever got about his onscreen smoking was a crank letter from someone who felt smokers' rights were being trampled on, and that portraying an evil character smoking wasn't fair.

All the actors I talked to agreed upon one thing: To smoke convincingly when acting, you have to have been a real-life smoker. Which it seems that most actors, for better or for worse, have been.

Chapter 20

FARCE

Throw a bunch of characters on a stage with an inordinate number of doors, create an improbable situation, raise the stakes impossibly high, toss in a few pratfalls, keep it all going at a fast clip, and you've got yourself a farce. "A comic dramatic piece that uses highly improbable situations, stereotyped characters, extravagant exaggeration, and violent horseplay," says *Encyclopedia Britannica.* How does an actor make this particularly outrageous form of comedy work? Are there any special *rules du genre,* so to speak?

Farce dates back to 15th-century France. It originally consisted of improvised buffoonery that actors stuck into the texts of religious plays; these bits were called *farce,* the Old French word for stuffing. Elements of farce—broad clowning, acrobatics—appeared in lots of plays after that, including those of Shakespeare and Molière, but nowadays when we think of farce we think mainly of Georges Feydeau's *A Flea in Her Ear* (1907), Brandon Thomas' *Charley's Aunt* (1892), and, from our own era, the works of Italian playwright Dario Fo, Ken Ludwig's *Lend Me a Tenor,* and Michael Frayn's *Noises Off.* Charlie Chaplin, the Marx Brothers, the Keystone Kops, Lucille Ball—all were consummate farceurs.

To succeed in farce requires a particular concentration and attention to detail and a willingness to commit totally and honestly to a ridiculous set of circumstances. It's been said that farce is very close to tragedy—and that's how seriously invested and larger-than-life you have to be about playing your intentions. Forget about being funny and just play the stakes for all they're worth, say the expert actors I consulted. In farce it's not the characters themselves that are funny, nor even the text (farce, traditionally considered lowbrow, usually lacks elevated dialogue and witty one-liners). Rather, the humor is in how the characters deal with the situation. And you better deal with it believably.

"Farce is no different than anything else," said Shashin Desai, who directed *Noises Off* in Long Beach, California. "It has to be honest and real. If what you're doing doesn't come from the character and the situation, if you're not grounded in what's happening, then it's not believable. You can have 100 funny beats. If you play nine of them over the top, it's a failure."

He added, "In farce you have to be a team player. If someone is trying to hog the spotlight, that would only happen at the expense of the play. Casting farce is a very difficult thing for a director. You look for actors with a sense of timing and working with others." Similarly, the director has to collaborate with the actors, allow them to bring in ideas, and nurture their talent, perhaps more so than in other theatrical forms. "There are two types of directors," opines Desai, "a father-instinct director and a mother-instinct director. The fathers demand, the mothers encourage and nurture." Farce, he believes, definitely calls for mothers.

One of his actors, Jodi Carlisle, said this was the hardest theatre piece she'd ever done, both physically (she soaked in a portable spa every night just to be able to walk the next day) and mentally. "Getting a feeling for the physicality of it was hard enough," she said. "But after that we had to go back to square one and realize these are real people, and we couldn't just do bits for bits' sake. Not trying to be funny, that was the hard part. When you hear laughter, the tendency is to do more and more. But you have to push the ego aside and focus on what's best for the piece." She observed that a lot of actors in farce tend to "put on the Three Stooges face, and it becomes about technique rather than reality."

Others agreed that making the audience laugh is mainly the job of the plot. Dan Hiatt, who appeared in another production of *Noises Off*, said that the director told the cast it was perfectly all right if the audience in the lobby after Act 1 was muttering, "Well, this isn't so funny." That has something to do with the particular three-act structure of *Noises Off*, an enormously clever play-within-a-play backstage farce with an elaborate set-up in Act 1 and a grand climax in Act 3. But the director was also reminding his actors about the necessity, in farce, to play it seriously. "You have to go logically, step by step, until the whole thing spirals out of control," said Hiatt. He used the inimitable John Cleese in *Fawlty Towers* as an example: "What he wants is the most important thing in the world to him. He's absolutely passionate." Similarly, said Hiatt, when you're in a farce, "you have to realize that what's happening is deadly serious and absolutely logical to the characters." He added, "Everything has to be driven by the story. There's a danger in getting outside of that. If it's well written, you can ride it like a roller coaster."

Sharon Lockwood echoed Hiatt's opinions. "Whether it's confusion of identities or whatever," she said, "in farce the comedy escalates and snowballs. Where it can go awry is if you're trying to graft something on that's not organic to the play." About to open in Ben Jonson's comedy *The Alchemist*, she noted that she and her fellow cast members, including such brilliant comic actors as Geoff Hoyle (of Broadway's *The Lion King*) and Ken Ruta, keep relearning the same lesson, and it's a lesson that also applies to farce: "Don't try to do bits. Just play the situation. It always goes back to that." One gesture, said Lockwood, is better than four or five in rapid succession. It's about "essentializing."

Nor can you rely on charm or general comic ability when you're in a farce, noted another veteran actor. Because you have so much physical business to deal with, you absolutely have to be specific, and you have to personalize. If necessary, you have to imagine the most extreme substitutions to make the high-stake nature of farce work for you in an authentic way. "If you're going to sell an improbable plot, you have to go for it 100 percent," he said. Farce is not the place for subtlety. Experience with outdoor acting helps with the kind of bigness you need. "Of course, in a smaller space you don't have to work so hard—but on the inside it has to be just as extreme."

Matthew Walker, in the Long Beach production of *Noises Off,* studied clowning with both the Ringling Brothers ("big and broad") and Bill Irwin ("relaxation and stillness"). That training helped him remember things like not hyperextending his hands when falling down a flight of stairs, which he did in Act 3. It also made him very aware of the technical requirements of farce. He said that old reruns of the TV show *Three's Company* offer a good example of exquisite timing of the sort that you need. "Whenever Jack would get hit in the face with a door, you knew when that door opened, he'd be making this priceless face."

From his physical training Walker also learned when too much is too much. "In my business with the phone in Act 3 of *Noises Off,* it would be easy to make it be about the phone—manipulating the phone cord, and so on," he said. "But it would be clowning for clowning's sake." On the other hand, he said, "There are places in Act 2 where during rehearsal we'd say, 'We have thirty seconds here and the author hasn't given us much, what would these characters do in this situation that's physical? And how are we going to vary it the third time to get the laugh?'" He believes there are times when you have to work out comic bits. His general advice is to not be afraid to take risks, to not be timid or tepid: "The playwright has created people who are a little more put-upon than normal. So the actor has to make strong choices and have a willingness to go with them."

But he offers warnings, too: "You have to be fully realized in every moment. It's really important that you're not just flying through, getting from a to z without going through b, c, and d."

For the Long Beach production of *Noises Off,* the cast had a three-week rehearsal with only four rehearsals on the actual set, with its demanding multiple levels and doors. "I think Frayn knew actors would be living this play whether they liked it or not," laughed Walker, noting that the onstage mishaps Frayn wrote into his play-within-a-play were reflected in reality as the actual cast members struggled to adjust their timing and deal with the detailed stage business in a too-short rehearsal period. All the actors were able to use those mortifying sense-memories in their acting.

Shashin Desai noted other dangers inherent to farce: "With dialogue comedy—for example, Noel Coward's *Private Lives*—you are safer; the dialogue carries you through. In farce if you raise your eyebrows too high, all of a sudden you're mugging." He added, you need good physical control, and, he reiterated, you absolutely have to be a team player. "If one person doesn't show up with the right prop, it doesn't matter how good an actor you are," because immediately everyone onstage is left hanging in the breeze.

Hanging in the breeze or not, playing farce is immensely rewarding. Most actors, said Walker, relish the heightened reality of the genre, so different from the usual theatrical fare, especially if you tend to do a lot of commercial work. "I think playwrights who write farces have been around actors," he said. "They know in a farce the actor's soul just lights up."

Chapter 21

DOCUDRAMA

There are two important things for actors to realize about working in docudrama: 1) The way you develop your character (or, in many cases, your multiple characters) will probably be radically different from what you're used to; and 2) you may find yourself bonded with your character in such a way that representing him or her respectfully is paramount; your actor's ego is virtually subsumed.

A genre popularized by Anna Deavere Smith's late-twentieth-century solo work—and seen in such shows as Eve Ensler's enormously successful *The Vagina Monologues*, Moises Kaufman's Tectonic Theatre Project work, and Mark Wolf's solo show *Don't Ask, Don't Tell*—docudrama involves a writer/director (who sometimes also performs the piece) interviewing subjects on a particular theme, using audio- and/or videotape. The material is transcribed, whittled down, organized, and workshopped. Finally a verbatim script emerges.

For Black Sheep/Encore Theatre Company's world premiere of *I Think I Like Girls* (an hour-and-forty-minute play about the lives of lesbians in America), writer/director Leigh Fondakowski recorded fifty interviews, two to five hours each, on audio- and videotape. (Fondakowski was also one of the main writers on Kaufman's original stage play, *The Laramie Project*, later filmed, about the effect of the brutal, homophobic Matthew Shepard murder on the ordinary citizens of Laramie, Wyoming.) Five women not only played the twenty roles but also participated actively in creating the piece.

Among the *Girls* ensemble was Kelli Simpkins, who was also in the cast of *The Laramie Project*. For the latter, she worked with audiotapes, transcripts, and Polaroid photos of the characters she played: a young lesbian activist, the boy who found Matthew Shepard, an older rancher, a Texas woman, and a young reporter named Tiffany. The project was workshopped at Sundance. "We listened to the tapes over and over," Simpkins told me. "We talked to several of the people who had conducted the interviews." On that project, actors too conducted some interviews. "Everyone came to the work in a different way. But once you hook in or connect with your characters, you kind of fall in love with them."

In fact, Simpkins was so concerned with representing her characters accurately that she initially went overboard, and, as she explained, "The actor/character dynamic became a little blurred for me." For example, she was persistent in trying to capture one character's high-pitched giggle, and it took her a long time, and repeated suggestions from the director, to start believing that sometimes the interviewee's precise physicality, behavior, and tics don't serve the play and the moment.

In a similar vein, in playing the young man who discovered Shepard, she found that the audiotape of his interview was fairly flat, too reflective. Simpkins eventually realized she was relying too much on the tape and needed to use her imagination to create the moment when the young man found the body. "I had to make it a theatrically urgent moment—put myself riding a bike down a mountain, find out how it would affect a young boy like him, other than how he was expressing it on tape. I think he was shell-shocked. I had to trust that I was being responsible and respectful with my presentation," she said. For Simpkins, responsibility and respect were overriding concerns in both projects. Fondakowski noted that actors in docudrama tend to have an extreme sense of ownership of their roles.

For actor Amy Resnick, the videotapes that Fondakowski made for *Girls* were invaluable, as were the accompanying audiotapes, which improved the quality of the voices when listened to on a Walkman. Resnick played six characters, all precisely differentiated and all deeply truthful.

"I started from the outside," she explained. With training in dance and Alexander as well as in the techniques of Stanislavski, Strasberg, and Stella Adler, Resnick tends to gravitate toward physical work, but such a complete outside-in approach was a departure even for her. "I approached it as a dancer," she said. "I'm an actor who dances, I work very much from my body. I usually find the walk of the character, how the character moves, and that helps me find the emotional life. [But] this process really involved mimicking. I didn't need to say what's my motivation? I started imitating the gestures I saw on the videotape moment by moment, verbatim. Also the intonation, where they placed their voice, the music and melody of the voice, the way their voice traveled up and down the scale. Different characters would hold their jaws differently, sit differently, play with their hair. What I found was quite magical. Suddenly you start to feel things. It's almost like channeling. You say it and then you figure out what you feel later. It's almost the British way of working. Just acting the music of Zackie's laugh, I went to this place of joy and openness. . . . Your own prejudices or stereotypical thoughts that you've formed because of your own life have to go aside."

Normally, explained Resnick, she would not have allowed herself to approach a role this way, fearing that it would be too overdone, too unbelievable. But here, the behavior of the actual person seen on videotape allayed her fears. She says she was able to achieve the moment-to-moment detail work toward which she'd always strived.

Acquiring those details is not easy. In *Girls,* the actors sometimes watched a single taped moment twenty times, dissecting it, looking for the one moment that defined the essence of the character. Resnick found herself scribbling minutely detailed notes in her script: "Her hand goes on her left knee." She compared the breadth of the work to musical instruments: whereas in the past she might have used a clarinet and a flute because those are the instruments she's familiar with, all of a sudden she found she had to pick up a French horn. Altogether, she said, it's like learning to drive a stick-shift. The movement eventually becomes second nature.

One of the techniques initiated by Kaufman and also used by Fondakowski requires specific homework for the actors: They brought in little solo or group improvs based on things they discovered about their characters, or impulses that came to them when studying the tapes; it's out of these "moment exercises" that the play evolved.

Doing all this, Resnick found that she was able to effectively get out of her own way and let the characters flow through her. "[Normally] you go to your stockpile," she said. "You know this is sexy, this is 'to convince,' you know how to play actions, all of that, but suddenly here you find yourself in a completely different sphere where you're sitting in a way you never sat before. I've worked Anne Bogart–style too, and I think her work is fascinating, but it often felt cold and automated. How do you bring humanity to that? That's what's extremely exciting about this work, how real and authentic and truthful it felt."

Simpkins added, "You don't have to imagine how your character sits or walks across the room, all that is taken care of. The work becomes about something else."

What exactly *is* it about? Although the process starts with superficial imitating, if approached with an open heart and flexible voice and body, it apparently works its way into your very core. In traditional plays, said Resnick, you work on your arc, your objective, actions. But for this work, "You have to be like an empty rice bowl, just a vessel for this person to come through. It's very freeing."

"There's that Brechtian twist," Simpkins elaborated. "The best performance is seeing the character and also seeing the actor. We're not trying to
become these people. It's a fine line between having the actor present and slipping into being too much the character. The answers are there for you: This
is how you sit, etc. But you still have to do the work of putting someone else's
body and voice into yours, and it's not easy."

Hard work it is indeed, but Resnick and Simpkins say there's nothing
like the experience of playing a real person. "I was an emotional wreck after
hearing Daphne's story," said Simpkins of the transgendered woman she
played in *Girls*. "I realized so many things about myself that I had never really
understood before. I had such a connection with her that I didn't want to
offend her [with my performance], I wanted the audience to applaud her. It
was an ethical position I was in, there was no actor ego involved.

"It's hard to think about doing a [traditional] play [after this]," she continued. "Part of me feels like I haven't done a play. I've been so moved,
changed, humanly challenged. Absolutely I will carry this with me for the rest
of my life as a human being and an actor. It's given me a feeling of power as a
person." In the androgynous role, Simpkins did indeed scarcely seem to be
acting. It's no wonder some in the audience thought she was the real Daphne.

Part of the enormous sense of responsibility comes from knowing the
interviewees may show up for the performance, a terrifying but ultimately
gratifying occasion for the actors. "The actual people become like icons," said
Fondakowski, "so when they're in the room, there's an incredible connection.
That's a great gift for actors, to be able to see the direct impact of their work,
the living presence of what that meant."

There are other, less cosmic, rewards of doing this kind of work. Resnick
believes the physical approach is helpful if you're in a situation—like a short
rehearsal period or a TV show—in which you have to come up with a character quickly. She was also able to use this physical way of working on a film,
Haiku Tunnel, by watching and imitating her kitten. "I've been afraid of doing
character work in film, I always think you've got to do something closer to the
bone, but I actually did character, and it really freed me up," she exulted.

Is this type of work for everyone? "If you're creatively inspired by your
imagination, this might not be the right kind of work for you," said Simpkins;
so much is proscribed from the get-go. Simpkins, who describes herself as not
a Method actor, finds that boundaries are ultimately freeing for her. "But if
you're a lover of research, and of the full spectrum of humanity, you'd love
this work. And if you really want to exercise your instrument—vocal, physical, dialect work—this is the pinnacle." She said playing Daphne has made her
grow as an actor and as a human being.

Resnick summed it up: "This work makes you look so much deeper than you normally do, very specifically and without judgment. What was extremely exciting about this work was how real and authentic and truthful it felt. I never felt like I'm acting. My actor's head is out of it. . . . You end up loving every one of these people."

Chapter 22

SHAKESPEARE

The famously tactless John Gielgud once remarked in the presence of that quintessential Falstaff, Orson Welles, "Have you ever known an American who could play Shakespeare?"—then added hastily, "Oh, Orson, I always thought you were Irish or something."

In a similar vein, critics have scoffed at Kenneth Branagh for adding American actors to the mix; remember the knocks he got for casting Jack Lemmon and Billy Crystal in his 1996 film *Hamlet?* But on the other hand, Dustin Hoffman triumphed as Shylock on the London stage in 1989. And what about such brilliant Shakespearean actors as Kevin Kline and Annette Bening?

The truth is, we Americans have long had an inferiority complex about our Shakespearean skills. Perhaps that's because the Bard isn't bred in our bones, so to speak, the way it is for the Brits; we're taught Shakespeare in school but somehow not as thoroughly as *they* are. When we start our conservatory training, we're still sweating over iambic pentameter and scansion; presumably our British counterparts have all those mechanics down pat early on.

As I discussed this whole topic with various Shakespearean actors and teachers, including some Brits and a few Americans who have studied Over There, a schism became apparent. Some of the pros believe that American actors need to work harder on the structural intricacies of the text. Others, however, think Americans are too intimidated by the poetry of the language, and they should stop worrying about it and get on with the usual tasks of the trade: character-building, objective-playing, etc.

Said James Newcomb, a veteran of various regional Shakespeare festivals, "We come from American psychological realism. We look for the personalized thing. Sometimes that tends to diminish [the material]. It becomes less about the language, the rhythm of the verse, which is undeniable." He elaborated: "You may have an instinct for how you feel about a moment, about what the language is saying, but it's just as crucial to know what the structure of the language is doing. [The language] is scored. More attention I think should be paid to that by American actors."

On the other hand, actor/university teacher Richard Easton asserted, "One doesn't have to fuss with the verse. When Tyrone Guthrie came to Stratford, Ontario, in the 1950s, he said that American actors are better equipped to play Shakespeare than the English, because they have so much energy, and their speech is closer to what Shakespeare's was." True enough. As Michael York explains in the foreword to Adrian Brine's *A Shakespearean Actor Prepares,* "The Elizabethan accent of Shakespeare's day [was] imported into America where it [took] root and flourished relatively intact. British English, on the other hand . . . suffered a significant sound change, along with a certain thespian gentrification." Sir Peter Hall has said that American actors are better equipped for Shakespeare precisely because our vowel sounds are closer to Shakespeare's than to Queen Elizabeth II's. Englishman Paul Whitworth, who has worked with the Royal Shakespeare Company, reminded me, "Nobody ever spoke like Shakespeare wrote." Indeed, Shakespeare coined 1,700 words for his plays.

Easton continued, "Shakespeare works wonderfully using American regional accents, particularly if they're sort of extreme and denote class and intelligence level, which is what English accents do." He said that when actors first read Shakespeare, "it's about spondees, meters, trochees, which is of no help. The actors are not reciting poetry. It's the play that's in verse. . . . The characters are not talking verse. You should work the same way you do with an Edward Albee play. Albee is very specific about the words, the punctuation. When he writes three dots, you've got to pause. The same is true with Shakespeare: You've got to obey the verse, keep the integrity of the lines—but that has nothing to do with your planning of who the character is." He added, "If you get spooky and dainty with it, it doesn't work."

Actor/director/teacher Julian Lopez-Morillas, though, spoke of the importance of the poetry. "Rhythm is particularly important in Shakespeare, in prose and especially in verse—essentially the interaction between underlying pulse in rhythm and verse and the melody of the words. You need to spend a good deal of time in that. . . . You have to understand [the text] through meaning, paraphrasing, dictionary work, as well as rhythm, scansion, and analysis of sound."

Countered Gwyneth Richards, who teaches "Shakespeare Without Tears," "Actors first approaching Shakespeare spend too much time in iambic pentameter, the scansion of a line. You cannot act a poetic line. You can act an objective, a relationship. You cannot act an iamb. When you scan a line, it remains in your mind and you speak [like you're reciting] a limerick. Scansion has nothing to do with acting; it's a poetic term for people who are into litera-ture. I've never had an acting class that talked about trochees or spondees."

Lopez-Morillas, though, did emphasize that he advocates working from both ends toward the middle: "Shakespeare never read Stanislavski! But that doesn't mean a Method approach is not valid. Ask yourself questions about objectives, given circumstances, but [at the same time] work with words, sounds, images." He noted, "We're conditioned to think of rhetoric and poetic values as somehow contradictory to psychological truth, but I think the opposite is true with Shakespeare. Scanning the lines, finding the music, reveal components of the psychological truth he's put into the text. You can't neglect either end."

Nor would Richards deny those elements. It's just, she explained, that you have to rely on Shakespeare, a canny actor himself, to do the work for you. "The words and the structure of the lines will give you the character," she advised. "Othello has long speeches with long o's and a's. If you go with that, the wail will be right there. Think of Lady Macbeth talking to her husband; she's just about slapping him around with the sounds of the words. You have to trust in it. . . . If you play the relationship, the motivation, the words fall naturally into place. If the character is moaning, the sounds of the words will moan. They will give you a clue how to say the speech, whether it's liquid, per-cussive . . . " She pointed out that in Shakespeare's day there was very little rehearsal time, and actors never saw the entire script, so they just had to go with it.

Oregon Shakespeare Festival's Michelle Morain clearly approaches her work from both ends. "It's vital to work on an honest portrayal of a human being and to honor the poetry of the language as well," she said. "You have to be willing to get out the dictionary, the special Shakespeare glossaries, figure out what you're saying, then figure out why. Just like with any play. Only it's more difficult, because so many of the words are no longer in use or have changed meaning. . . . When you first practice saying the language, it feels so funny in your mouth, you feel stilted and self-conscious, because we have such a pallid verbal situation in everyday speech. You start feeling hoity-toity. But the more you practice, the more natural it feels."

So what do British actors think of it all? I once took a Scottish actor guest to see a local production of *Romeo and Juliet*. "It's like watching *L.A. Law!*" she marveled, of the American accents. She was also surprised at the way the actors so clearly articulated every word. British actors, she said, sound much more conversational, less staccato. But she added that she actually achieved a new understanding of parts of the text (and she'd seen *R & J* at least ten times previously) because of the American style. And Californian Chris Ayles, a Brit who trained privately in England in the '60s, commented, "Americans, taught Shakespeare at universities, learn the poetry, the language, the iambic pentameter. Over there, we're taught that Shakespeare wrote dialogue just like any other playwright. We study it just like you study David Mamet." In fact, a Juilliard-trained co-actor in *Twelfth Night,* a show he was in at the time, said she wanted to make her own speech sound more modern and natural, the way Ayles' did.

Ayles identifies a rote "da *dum* da *dum* da *dum* da *dum* da *dum*" rhythm in American actors' speech. "Shakespeare as played at Stratford is easy to understand," he explained, "because they're just *talking* to each other."

American Conservatory Theater's dialect teacher, Deborah Sussel, said, "We Americans tend to overstress words. We plod through our speech. That's fine for American plays, but when dealing with Shakespeare's verse, it becomes critical to de-emphasize certain syllables for iambic pentameter."

Sussel was dialect coach for a production of *Cymbeline* in which the director worked with the text the way he'd been taught by Peter Hall, taking a little caesura at the end of every line of verse, never pausing in the middle of the line. Sussel noted that the cast found this difficult: American actors are used to pausing whenever they want. However, Sussel herself was trained by the legendary Bill Ball, who, she said, spoke metaphorically of "riding the horse of the verse" to the end—the technique, said Sussel, that's been taught to generations of British actors.

In the '80s Robert Vincent Frank, now an Oregon Shakespeare Festival veteran, arrived from America for a three-year program at the Guildhall School of Music and Drama in London. He was expecting a traditional approach, but instead, "It was very much about the contemporary idea of the Method." Students worked first and foremost on finding the psychological truth of the character. The vocal department was run at the time by the famous Patsy Rodenburg, who said, "We will not spend time looking at scansion or iambic pentameter. I assume you know all about that. When you deliver the text onstage, the audience won't care about that." This demystified British training for Frank.

Frank believes that American actors, influenced by Strasberg's interpretation of Stanislavski's teachings, probably delved into psychological truth onstage earlier than did the Brits. He also noted that in the '50s, Paul Robeson was the first black man to play Othello (opposite Uta Hagen). "Even before the British, we did Shakespeare as a contemporary," he said. "It's part of our culture, the way we've evolved. I credit the whole Method school for that."

Just as British training was demystified for Frank at Guildhall, so was it simplified for Alexandra Matthew, an American who spent a year at the Drama Studio London. But the lessons she brought home were slightly different. "I learned in England to let the words work on me rather than me put emotions on top of the words," she said. "If I dissect the words, the rhythm of the line, the character will emerge through me rather than me trying to be this great character. One of my teachers said, 'There is no Lady Anne out there.' She only exists in how I speak her. This was just as much news to the Brits as to me."

Matthew said that both her British and her American training (at Brown University) de-emphasized the verse. Nevertheless, she learned that there is a reason why a particular word is at the end of a particular verse line. "You might emphasize that word with a stress or with intonation or take a little beat," she said. "You don't have to, but the opportunity is there to find out, what did Shakespeare intend here? We tend to read it as if it were prose to make it more accessible, and it kills some of the power." But she also learned in London that if a line is simple, say it simply. Look for places where lines can be thrown away.

I saw Paul Whitworth play Macbeth at Shakespeare Santa Cruz (where he is artistic director, actor, and professor at the University of California, Santa Cruz). I noted—as I did once when watching a touring production of the RSC's *The Taming of the Shrew*, and as I always do when seeing McKellen, Dench, Jacobi, Branagh, Maggie Smith, et al. in British Shakespeare films—how at ease he was with the language. Yet his acting was powerfully psychologically based, just like the best of his American co-actors in *Macbeth*.

"The contrasts between American and British actors are exaggerated," he told me. "In England, you hear that American actors are more physical, which I don't believe. Nowadays in England, everyone does a bit of screen work, so the distinctions are blurring."

Deborah Sussel concurred, saying, "I don't think there's much difference between what's taught to British actors and what we teach at A.C.T. Playing intentions and actions—all that comes from Stanislavski and is taught in both countries when teaching Shakespeare. Heightened language is the older tradition. The new tradition is naturalistic acting. The two have to be married."

As is clearly seen from all these varying opinions and viewpoints, every actor, whether British or American, reflects his or her specific training. There's apparently no common language among actors in approaching Shakespearean text—which, as one director complained, presents quite a challenge in pulling together a cohesive cast.

Whitworth's main concern is that on both sides of the Atlantic the striving for individuality, and distinctive artistic style, is taking the place of careful text analysis. His advice for actors? "Beware of fancy techniques. Treat Shakespeare like any other great dramatist. Know the play well before you start. Read lots of Shakespeare." He added, "The most important thing is genuine imagination, which is a private matter. I learn my lines before rehearsal begins. That way private work goes on where Shakespeare meets your own world. The quiet relation between the actor and the text is the most sacred thing to the actor's imagination. You can roll with the punches if you're alive inside."

Michelle Morain has another concern that further expands the discussion: "If we want to create and maintain audiences into the future, they need to start hankering after Shakespeare," she said. "And I don't think they can do that unless they understand it has something to do with them and life today, that these characters are human people experiencing jealousy, grief, fear."

"My personal feeling," declared Lopez-Morillas, "is that Shakespeare's greatest strength is his character creation, and poetry is secondary to that."

I'll add, from my own experiences watching both American and British actors perform Shakespeare, that what makes the bottom-line difference between being drawn into a production or feeling distanced from it is not whether the actors have a good handle on the poetry, but rather whether the characters are full and human. For that sense of personal truth, your nationality doesn't matter one farthing's worth.

Chapter 23

PINTER

Those famous ... pauses; the mystery-and-menace quotient; the edgy, comic tone; the gritty, musical language; the characters' erratic behavior: Acting in the plays of Harold Pinter is a challenge. (Americans have the additional, unavoidable burden of the British accents, which are inextricably woven into the fabric of the text.)

Andrew Robinson, who directed *The Birthday Party* at Los Angeles' Matrix Theatre, effectively conveyed the quintessential elusiveness of Pinter this way: Stanley lives in a boarding house. You don't know why. You don't know the nature of his relationship with Meg and Petey except that he's their boarder. But he hasn't paid any rent for a year. So there's something else going on. You don't know why Goldberg and McCann are there. Are they looking for Stanley? It's up to the audience, said Robinson, to attach meaning to these situations and characters.

Likewise, the actors must personalize their characters' behavior. "If the actors do not fill their characters and the subtextual world of their characters with their [own] story, then the audience doesn't have a chance," warned Robinson.

Pinter requires high-stakes objectives, loaded subtext, a comic sensibility (while never playing for laughs), a willingness to be hated by the audience, an in-the-moment flexibility and aliveness, a non-naturalistic style, a deep emotional connection (otherwise it's parody, cautioned American Conservatory Theater artistic director Carey Perloff), and more. Yet, like Shakespeare, Pinter—also an actor—writes consummately actable plays.

Pinter's signature language is similar—in its rhythms and terse banalities—to David Mamet. For Lawrence Pressman, who played Goldberg in the Matrix's *The Birthday Party*, the rhythms—including the patterns of the text on the page—provide endless clues. He gave me an example, using Goldberg and McCann's first four lines:

McCann: Is this it?

Goldberg: This is it.
McCann: Are you sure?
Goldberg: Sure I'm sure.

"Look at the repeats alone!" exclaimed Pressman. "That's very musical, rhythmic, imagistic. It's really prose poetry that's so rare in theatre that when you get it, it's gold. Pinter is like a wonderful score that you then have to fill. You can't start with your internal workings and not start with the text at the same time, because if you do, you'll suddenly get to the stage where you've got all these words and you don't know what they mean." He thinks of Pinter's text as being a mixture of Bach ("with this whole other world that you can't quite hear") and jazz ("totally in the moment").

Added Pressman's co-actor Robert Symonds, who played Petey, "I think Pinter labored over each word and where it's placed. You need to be quite precise. You can't leave out syllables." Symonds, a seasoned vet, played Goldberg in the American premiere of *The Birthday Party* at San Francisco's Actors' Workshop in 1960.

"This is a very different world from O'Neill," Perloff observed. When I talked to her, she was fresh from directing a sterling production of two Pinter one-acts, *The Room* (his earliest) and *Celebration* (his latest). "Pinter characters use language to skewer each other," explained Perloff. "American actors tend to use language confessionally rather than combatively. And nothing in Pinter is confessional. . . . You have to know who you're sending every line to, and what its effect is going to be." Pinter wrote that in his plays, speech "is a constant stratagem to cover nakedness."

Perloff described the rehearsal process for *Celebration*. "These are two couples who loathe each other. So we'd do a run-through where all this loathing comes through—nastiness, despair. Then you have to cover it. These people have been married for twenty-five years. They have strategies to deal with how they feel about each other. They use their language to skewer each other in a comic way that allows them to survive." In other words, in rehearsing, the actors first discovered the feelings behind the mask, then put on the mask.

According to Pressman—who was directed by the playwright himself in *The Man in the Glass Booth* in London and New York in the late '60s, with Donald Pleasance and Robert Shaw—Pinter said that if you merely emphasize certain words in any speech and don't worry about the meaning, you will find yourself using speech "as a weapon, a cover, a wooing device, a beating of a fist upon a door."

To justify that extreme use of language, you need a strong objective. Perloff has written (in a subscriber newsletter), "There is nothing casual or low-key in a Pinter play. It is a violent act to walk into a room, to knock on a door. So you make strong choices about what the characters want: Haven? Comfort? Dominance? Power? The things they want are in explosive conflict with the things desired by other characters, which makes the actions enormous: I want to colonize . . . destroy you . . . make love to you. There is no middle ground in Pinter. You're either predator or prey."

When I talked to Perloff, she elaborated: "It has to be clear what you want, what you're trying to do to someone else, and where the wound is. Very literally. These are always characters with wounds." She added that ultimately the objective for a Pinter character is to survive.

Robinson amended that: "The other objective is connecting. These characters—certainly in *The Birthday Party* and *The Homecoming* [which Robinson has also directed]—are often in removed, alienated situations and are trying to connect. In *The Homecoming,* when Ruth comes to the home of Max and his brother and son, the dramatic event is how she recognizes their hunger and finds she is needed and chooses to stay, sending her husband back to America. In *The Birthday Party* Meg has such a need for Stanley. And Stanley has a great need to connect with Meg and Petey. Whether they do or not is a whole other thing." For Robinson, it's useful to find a spine for each character similar to the spine of a commedia or restoration comedy character. In commedia, for example, such stock figures as il Dottore, Arlecchino, etc., each have a powerful life objective, or spine.

Pressman creates a biography for his characters. Whatever is said on the page about the character's past, he has a concurrent running story that is sometimes the same, sometimes the opposite, and sometimes entirely unrelated.

Inevitably, your objective (and other choices you make) will fuel your subtext. Pinter wrote, "There are two silences. One when no word is spoken. The other when perhaps a torrent of words is being employed. This speech is speaking of a language locked beneath it."

"If you don't have a subtext in Pinter, you're lost," said Robinson. "Like an elevator with no car. You'll freefall down the shaft." He went on, "There's fear and terror and secrets in *The Birthday Party*. To give the dramatic sense of secrets you have to *have* secrets. 'I the actor am not going to tell you the audience and you the other actors what's going on in my life, what I'm playing.' Otherwise, nothing is at stake."

On the other hand, Pressman sees the subtext issue slightly differently. He remembers reading that a director once told Laurence Olivier that Shakespearean acting is never done under the line—that is, you can't subtext it to death—and you can't act over the line—you can't be overwrought about it. You have to be in the dead center of the line, and the line expresses your intention. "I can't think of another playwright about whom that is so true except with Harold," mused Pressman.

Still, there's no denying that your subtext is a large part of what's going on during those obligatory "pauses" and "silences" that so confound actors. (A frustrated Ralph Richardson once asked Pinter how many pauses make a silence, and Pinter responded, "Three or four." Make of that what you will.)

"When you first begin to work on a Pinter script," wrote Perloff, "you won't know why the silence is there. So you simply have to honor that silence and hold it until it begins to fill. It's in those silences that you realize the depth of the characters' loneliness, their need for love . . ."

I asked her if the pauses and silences always fell in the right places, and she said, "If the stakes are high and the language detonates the way it should, the pauses that are scripted are absolutely necessary and you know them when you find them. Pinter is an actor and knows where the bottom drops out and where someone makes a radical left turn." Those moments are exactly where the pauses are. In the A.C.T. production, the pauses were so organically interwoven that I didn't register them as such, which is as it should be.

"Harold says it can be a breath or an honest-to-goodness stop," reported Pressman. "It's an end of something, but out of that end comes a beginning of something else." He studies the pauses and silences as if they were speeches. "When a character gets to his real core, he has no choice but to go into silence or pause. To me that's where the plays live," added Pressman.

"His plays are so actable," wrote Perloff, "because they're so incredibly, vividly, moment to moment. . . . a Pinter character only exists the moment he or she hits the stage. Just as, when a new person walks into your life, they only begin to exist for you at that moment."

Pressman agreed. "You must re-create the play from the ground up every time. You bring in that day's wound, that life's wound, every time. You can't go on automatic." He is almost mystical about the experience of playing Pinter: "You're actively fucking and being fucked at the same time. It is the oddest experience I've ever had. I don't know how to talk about it—an inner sensation that is both passive and aggressive at the same time. Sometimes one overcomes the other. If you try to control it, it will bite you." He knows what each word of the script means to his character and, more personally, to himself, the actor behind the character, "but I don't lock myself into any of that. What makes it scary is you must be creative every single time."

Along with staying alive in the moment, the Pinter actor faces startling transitions. As Symonds described it, you go from point A to point B with nothing in between. "You have to accept that and learn how to do it," he said. Onstage life takes place at warp speed, so transitions from one emotion or attitude adjustment to the next get compacted.

Pinter told Perloff that actors need not carry the emotional freight from one moment to the next. "A bomb is dropped and detonates and you move on," said Perloff. "It's a very different kind of work from the way actors are taught in this country, where one thing invariably leads to the next. It's a more jagged, unpredictable landscape."

Jagged, unpredictable, as mysterious as . . . life itself. In fact, said Perloff, "Pinter feels it's a kind of arrogance on the part of a playwright or director or actor to have an airtight story about where somebody comes from and what their motivations are, because we don't even know that about ourselves." Creating an elaborate backstory for your character may not be helpful in a Pinter play, Perloff suggested.

And don't concern yourself with symbols, either. Symonds, who was in the American premiere of the one act *Landscape* with Mildred Natwick, on a double bill with *Silence*, remembers one actor asking Pinter, who sat in during some rehearsals, "Is he sort of a symbol of death?" No, said Pinter, he's just a very old man.

Many years ago Pinter explained his work to Pressman this way: "Imagine there's a hotel room next door with people in it. You bore a hole in the wall and everything you see through that hole is my play. You can't see anything to the left or right. If a character moves away from the hole, you're left with blackness for a while, or another character appears."

This was enlightening for Pressman, who also offered some advice on how to initially approach the script: See what the patterns on the page look like. Do they mean anything to you? Look at them like an abstract work of art. Then get into the saying of them, and speak them faster initially than you might, get them trippingly on your tongue. Then let them go deep into your soul. Stop on individual words and let them wash over you. Let them be. See if they bring up an image and follow that image and see if that image creates another image.

Robinson said it's helpful for actors to work from the outside in as much as from the inside out when creating their characters—you're not dealing with Arthur Miller or Tennessee Williams here, he noted—and to have an affinity for paradox and ambiguity: A character could be lying and/or telling the truth at any given moment. "For every choice you make as the character, there's an opposite choice," said Robinson. "You're always going towards and against your objective at the same time. The danger is in getting hung up on the literalness of your questions and trying to establish a logic; Pinter will always defy you. Most of the time the questions are more valuable than the answers."

Chapter 24

MOLIÈRE

Before undertaking a Molière play, it's helpful to know something about the enormously popular 17th-century French comic playwright. Born Jean-Baptiste Poquelin in Paris, son of a successful tradesman, he left his social class for the lowly life of an actor. Acting, writing, directing, and managing his own theatre company, he ultimately found favor in the court of Louis XIV.

Many of Molière's characters—in such plays as *The Miser, Tartuffe,* and *The Imaginary Invalid*—and plots were drawn from the Italian commedia tradition.

Although he started out writing farces, Molière eventually turned to comedy of manners. "His innovation was the brilliance of his language and his psychological perceptions," said Brian Bedford, who directed and acted in a double bill of *The School for Husbands* and *The Imaginary Cuckold* at the Mark Taper Forum. "He replaced the improv of commedia with quite brilliant organized text."

It's important to know that Molière wrote most of the leading roles for himself. As such, the main characters reflect his own deepest obsessions, his struggles with religious hypocrisy, greed, etc. The rest of the roles were written for members of his troupe. Noted Carey Perloff, artistic director of American Conservatory Theater, "All these plays were written for the same actors, and once you know that, and understand what their relationships were to each other, it's really fun."

"All Molière's protagonists are people with tremendous psychological problems," Bedford told me. "Molière, like Chekhov, found neurotic complications funny." Bedford too finds these "complex, neurotic, self-involved, frightened, insecure people" funny.

Molière's characters are indeed exaggerated, and they each tend to have a single obsessive trait. Thus playing your objective to the hilt is a requirement. Joan Holden, longtime San Francisco Mime Troupe playwright who has adapted Molière, said, "Actors need to understand that you don't ask yourself what their childhood experiences were. These characters are driven by deep id drives." When working on an adaptation and translation of *The Imaginary Invalid* at Denver University, Holden saw that the actors gradually had to learn to trust how simple the characters in that play are. "They all want something: love, attention, money," she said. "If the actor plays that, everything else takes care of itself because the writing is so great. Where an actor gets in trouble is in trying to complicate the characters. They're rich characters, but they're not complicated." She used, as an example, Argan, the main character in *Invalid:* "He's essentially Pantelone—he's worried about money, selfish, a hypochondriac, a maniac. But at the same time he has a middle-class father's affection for his children. You love him because Molière writes so deeply his fears and his passions that you identify with him." Holden recalled René Auberjonois' Tartuffe at A.C.T. in 1967: "I can still feel the fire of his lust, more than thirty years later!" That's just how strong and pure your objectives need to be.

Observed Dakin Matthews, who starred as Arnolphe in *School for Wives* at South Coast Repertory, "The difficulty for American actors raised in Stanislavski is that they want to make it natural, and you can't. The act of the actor performing this character is what makes it real. If you're really behaving that way, the audience accepts it as real."

Matthews noted a difficulty he had in preparing to play Arnolphe: "*School for Wives* is Molière's first step toward grand comedy, but he still has one foot in commedia. So sometimes this character acts in a modern psychological way and other times like a Pantelone-type commedia character. Half of him is from 14th-century Italian comedy and the other half 17th-century grand comedy. Because he's so schizoid, it works. But it's not naturalistic; it's theatrical and theoretical."

He added, "Trust the language and focus on the objective. The characters are always tremendously energetic, and, because many of them are based on Molière's own psychology, they are somewhat self-revealing. . . . Don't tone down the character to fit a picture you have of human behavior."

To play your objectives as fully as the text demands, you must look within yourself and then magnify what you find there 200 times. "Molière exaggerates common vices of mankind: lust, greed, misanthropy, hypocrisy," said Matthews. "We all have a touch of these." It goes without saying that you mustn't try to be funny.

So that's the psychology—simple enough. As for the language: "These alexandrines [twelve syllables per line of verse] in which Molière wrote [some but not all of his plays] had to have alternate masculine and feminine endings in addition to the rhymes," noted Bedford. Yet, he argued, Molière was not highfalutin and poetic but rather "the thinking man's fun." We English speakers are most familiar with Richard Wilbur's translations of Molière's plays. In the verse plays, Wilbur retained the verse in English. Holden believes this presents an acting obstacle. It's easier to rhyme in French, she pointed out, so the French version sounds closer to natural speech than do Wilbur's verse translations. English-language actors risk becoming sing-songy.

Some companies do non-Wilbur translations—South Coast Rep's *Wives* was translated by Ranjit Bolt, a Brit, and it still has rhyming couplets, but Matthews said the meter is less rigid than is Wilbur's. However, there were a lot of Britishisms in the translation that had to be reworked for the South Coast Rep production.

When A.C.T. staged *The Misanthrope*, Perloff commissioned playwright Constance Congdon to adapt a new translation, mainly in order to take a deeper look at the often-trivialized character of Célimène (based on Molière's wife). Congdon's version rhymed, too.

So how to get comfortable with the verse? Matthews advised, "Don't hit the rhymes unless you'd hit them if they *weren't* rhymes. You have to think about it, make it your own, and then let it slip into your subconscious. Be aware when it is and isn't important for the audience to hear the rhyme. If it's the clinch line of a joke, you want it to be heard."

Bedford, a close friend and associate of Richard Wilbur, suggested initially ignoring the rhyming couplets. "Go with the colloquial meaning and speaking of the text. Then at some point you have to bear in mind that there are rhythms that cannot be ignored." As Matthews noted, "Having audiences hear the rhymes is part of the fun." But, he warned, "You cannot let the verse ride you. It's a thoroughbred and will take you where you want to go, but you've got to ride it, not let it ride you."

Of course Molière presents more to deal with, language-wise, than the verse. In fact, Matthews said that more important than understanding rhyme or meter is understanding the rhetorical structure of the long speeches, "learning how a thought develops over a period of twenty to thirty lines or more—the principles of composition.... Molière is pretty empty of metaphor [unlike Shakespeare]," he continued, "but structure of speech, logic, how thoughts connect to each other—you can see with extreme specificity the beginning and end of a speech and how the character's mind goes from beginning to end." Analyzing the structure of the speeches makes it easier to memorize them, because you're memorizing thought length as well as words. Another benefit is that when you make choices for the sake of variety within the long speeches, your choices will be logical, not arbitrary. If you don't understand the structure of the speech, you may be fast where you should be slow, or loud where you should be soft.

It's also important to acquire the lung capacity for the long speeches. "You can't take pauses where *you* feel like you want to pause, but rather where the *language* wants you to pause," explained Matthews. Bedford, who studied speech with John Gielgud, said, "You need to have a good, strong voice that's capable of a great deal of variety of tone and pitch, capable of manifesting contrasting thoughts to serve the musicality of the text. I learned from John the necessity of variety in these long speeches."

"The language is very taut and arch, and underneath it's a play filled with longing and the desire for love," said Perloff, of *The Misanthrope*. "The collision of those two things is really interesting." She emphasized that the language, while not naturalistic, is beautifully crafted as part of the action of the play.

Assuming you've had some classical training, here are a few suggestions for acquiring additional expertise:

Dakin Matthews thought the study of 17th-century rhetoric would be helpful although not necessary—you'll begin to get a grounding in it during rehearsals. He also said that it's important to immerse yourself in reading, and in language in general. "Language has to be like oxygen, natural and vital to your whole body. You have to live in an oxygen-enriched atmosphere to maintain the energy and precision you'll need."

"Immerse yourself in the period—the art, the costumes," recommended Bedford. "Read about the characteristics of the people. You are successful with Molière's verse plays to the extent that you make the language come to a vibrant, contemporary life."

Perloff, in rehearsing *The Misanthrope*, had her cast look at visual material of the era. "You can tell from the shape of the clothes how people stood. Then you ask, what does it mean for a man to stand with his legs turned out that way? What kind of man would do that? What does that say about his behavior?" She also recommended listening to Handel and baroque opera, looking at visual imagery of the architecture, and reading letters written in that period.

Lastly, said Matthews, "Don't ignore the audience. They are part of the experience in plenty of the monologues, which are directed at them."

By the way, ironically enough, Molière collapsed during a performance of his last play, *The Imaginary Invalid*, and died later that same night.

Chapter 25

MULTIPLE ROLES

If you've acted in summer stock or rep, you've probably been asked by at least one admiring and clueless fan, "Do you ever get confused about what play you're in and say the wrong lines?" Well, of course you don't. No actor would. Similarly, if you're playing multiple roles within one play—which, usually for budgetary rather than artistic reasons, is very common these days, especially with the classics—you can rest assured you won't ever enter spouting the dialogue of the wrong character. Nevertheless, when cast in two or more roles in a production you'll find there are special challenges.

To take the most extreme example possible: In a stripped-down and hysterically funny version of Shakespeare's *The Comedy of Errors* that I saw, five actors played sixteen roles—*and* they crossed genders, *and* each of the two sets of identical twins was played by a single actor.

For Susannah Schulman, who played both Antipholus of Ephesus and Antipholus of Syracuse, this wasn't the first time she'd played multiple roles. In the national tour of Steve Martin's *Picasso at the Lapin Agile* she played Suzanne, the young woman looking for Picasso; the Countess (Einstein's date for the night); and a rabid "female admirer." But in *Picasso* the costumes pretty much did the work for her in terms of delineating characters. Also she was able to focus most of her attention on the role of Suzanne, since the other two parts were much smaller (and no, she doesn't feel that doing the extra roles detracted from working on Suzanne). And in *A Christmas Carol* at South Coast Rep, she played a variety of small roles, including two clear polar opposites: the ladylike Belle, and a lowly street person.

But in this flapper-era *Errors,* playing identical twins, she wore identical costumes, right down to the matching straw boaters, with only a pair of glasses to distinguish the two Antipholi. The rest was up to her actorly skills, although the director helped by assigning Southern accents to all Syracusans and New York accents to all Ephesians.

The important thing that Schulman discovered was that if she made a physical choice for one character—and distinctive physical choices, including vocal choices, are crucial for this type of work—the other character couldn't ever do anything remotely comparable. "In getting into the character of Syracuse, I'd put my hands in my pockets, and think, yes, this feels good, this feels like him. But then Ephesus can't *ever* put his hands in his pockets, that's too relaxed for him. Whereas if I were just playing Ephesus, maybe he could put his hands in his pockets." Even more so than in playing a single role, you have to justify—you have to determine *why* Ephesus doesn't ever put his hands in his pockets, not something you'd necessarily have to consider in other circumstances. Schulman's Syracuse was self-confident, he stood back on his heels, chest out; the more uptight Ephesus had hunched shoulders.

This *Comedy of Errors* was the most physical show Schulman had ever done. So during rehearsals she closely observed another cast member, the versatile Joan Mankin, who's worked with the San Francisco Mime Troupe, the Pickle Circus, and other great physical comedy groups. In fact, touring with Dell'Arte Players Company, she once appeared as three different characters in each play of a trilogy—which at times was performed in its entirety, so that Mankin played nine different roles in one evening—"my best experience of all time!" she declared.

In *Errors*, Mankin played the decrepit Egeon as well as Doctor Pinch and the goldsmith Angelo. The first thing she did was get a general idea of the physicality of the three—and because of all the circusy roles she's played, that approach comes naturally to her. "It's all about the way I stand and my voice," she said. "I get up there and put my body in different positions until it feels right. It's intuitive." Unlike Schulman, she had three different costumes and wigs, not to mention assorted facial hair, for the three men, although that made for some mighty quick costume changes.

"Danny gave me clues," said Mankin, referring to the director, Danny Scheie. "He told me the goldsmith is low status, trying to get to the top, a whiner, so that made me hunch my shoulders." Dr. Pinch was more problematic, but during a read-through Mankin suddenly visualized the whiskery face of New Age health guru Dr. Andrew Weil and seized upon that image for what turned out to be a hilariously sleazy character with a swagger. Egeon, on the other hand, is bent over with age. She experimented with voices, too: The goldsmith's ended up high and nasal; the doctor, whom she conceived as rather slimy, had oily tones.

"Don't attempt to go too deeply at first, but rather first get the outlines of the characters," Mankin advised. "Find a way to get in and out of character quickly. Then work on it from the inside. You are presenting a sketch [of the character] in a way."

Schulman, on the other hand, approached each role exactly the way she would a single character. "Actors all play different roles all the time," she said. "Playing them in the same production is just an extension of that." But don't forget to make sure the different characters don't share any physical mannerisms. Added Schulman, "The more I developed each one as an individual, the more their voices took on their characteristics. If you prepare each role as completely and specifically as you would if it were your only role, then you can't go wrong."

Danny Scheie, known for his fevered directorial imagination, also cast some of the actors in multiple roles and across genders when he directed *The Merchant of Venice.* That included one actor playing both Shylock and Lorenzo (who steals Shylock's daughter). "It shows up the father-son thing," commented Scheie, "and also the anti-Semitism of the play, and criticizes it a little bit. I think doubling can make audiences think in real ways. It forces both the actors and the audience to ask smarter questions." With his antic *Errors,* which he'd directed several times prior to the production that Mankin and Schulman were in, he didn't hide the fact that some of the actors were playing several roles; sometimes they even changed costumes onstage. "In theatre, no matter how realistic it is, there's the awareness that the actor is playing a role," he said. "When you stumble, it makes it more magical."

As an actor, Scheie has played multiple roles himself, including a young gay man and a colonial housewife in Caryl Churchill's *Cloud 9* at Berkeley Rep; the infamous *The Mystery of Irma Vep* in which two actors play a myriad of personae; and four roles in *The Imaginary Invalid* at Yale Rep, including a ten-year-old girl. Like Schulman and Mankin, he loves the challenge. "I use a lot of myself in each character," he explained. He thinks the acting needs to be broader and bolder if you're playing several roles. "You can't be too subtle. And costume changes aren't enough. Find the split personality within you and take it all the way." He added, "You have to do more storytelling rather than the selfish, this-is-all-about-me type of acting."

That brings up another important point about playing multiple roles: You get to see the broader arc of the play because you're not immersed in just one character's POV. You can see what the play needs in a way that you can't when you're locked into one persona. That increased awareness will influence your artistic choices.

And you're also, as Mankin pointed out, presenting yourself to the audience more as an actor than as the character. The contract you might normally have with an audience—the agreement that for the time being you *are* the character—is broken. In *Errors,* Mankin sensed the audience looking at her and trying to figure out who she was. "It's a funny distancing technique," she observed. She agreed that it sometimes prevents the audience from taking the characters too seriously—which, in *Comedy of Errors,* is perfectly all right. No doubt it can be problematic in a drama, where you don't want the audience to be distracted in a way that's detrimental to the play.

Of course there are tense moments. One night Mankin suddenly found herself as Egeon standing with her hands and feet in the posture of Pinch (a sort of fifth-ballet position, with evenly balanced weight; her lecherous Pinch "always knows where his pelvis is"). "I panicked," she said. "I don't know how my feet got there; Egeon is so different from Pinch, Egeon's old and sometimes he staggers." Most of the time, though, "you kind of get it into your bloodstream when you're going to be making an entrance. If you're not standing where you're supposed to be to come on, you can't breathe because you're not there. It's a different thing to be standing and waiting as three different people rather than just as one."

And Schulman despaired during early rehearsals when she found herself slipping back and forth between the two regional accents. But that problem cleared up as soon as she got into the real work.

All three agreed that playing multiple roles is a bonanza for an actor. "It puts actors in their element," said Schulman. "There's maybe this tiny molecular restructuring within your body, but it doesn't take a great amount of effort. It comes naturally. It asks us to do what we're here to do, in a microcosm."

This is an opportunity you'll never get in film, as Scheie pointed out. "Here's a chance to buck your type, break out of the pigeonhole, maybe for good. Don't play it safe," he counseled.

Chapter 26

SCRIPT ANALYSIS

In the beginning, there is the playwright. Then there is you. When the playwright and you, the actor, merge, when the playwright's words and your innermost self—your memories and thoughts and feelings—connect, the result is what we call a "character." It's as simple as that. Script analysis is a useful first step in the process of creating the character.

So says San Francisco acting teacher Jean Shelton. I sat in on a few sessions of her script analysis class to get a brief overview of the process she has put together to analyze scripts, which she herself learned from Stella Adler.

When you respect the playwright's moment-by-moment work, Shelton believes, you will be able to simplify your own job as an actor, because you'll find that your other actorly tasks will follow naturally. Script analysis, she told the class, is neither psychoanalytical thinking nor English-major thinking. Already I was surprised. I'd always assumed that script analysis involved a scholarly approach to the text. Not so. Script analysis means understanding what the play is about, understanding what is happening in each scene, and then zeroing in on your character to find out why she is saying and doing the things she says and does when she says and does them.

"In the theatre," explained Shelton, "the lines are about more than they are in real life, even though the play's style might be natural. The lines are the tip of the iceberg. They say, 'Go this way.' . . . You start with what the writer gives you, and you use your understanding of yourself to match the writer. The playwright and the actor become one, and move as a unit. Both you and the playwright have something you want to communicate. The playwright is your partner."

This type of work presupposes, of course, that you've done enough introspection to be in touch with your deepest self. Clearly, the best playwrights have done so.

It also presupposes—and this, said Shelton, is very important—that you do not judge your character, that you are open-minded and willing to motivate and justify all your character's words and actions. "Don't worry about what the other characters in the play say about your character," she cautioned, and this is clearly an anti-English-major viewpoint, and probably contrary to what most acting teachers advise. "You're only responsible to your character. Believe what *your* character says! Get behind your character!" The rest is up to the director and the audience.

How do you support, and not prejudge, your character? By delving deeply enough into your own experiences and observations of people and the world around you to identify with her. Not prejudging is trickier than it sounds, Los Angeles actor Wendy Phillips told me. "Actors tend to start seeing themselves and imposing their character on the script." The idea is to initially let the script work on you, not you work on it. "I try not to even judge the way I'm reading it," said Phillips. "I have to get through it five times, any way, any how." She added, "They say there are five main stories in literature. Probably a good actor has three stories. If you don't let the [author's] story work on you, you'll end up telling your same three stories. And it'll get dull."

Let's get down to basics. First, *read the play* at least twice. Different actors have different ways of dealing with that first, solitary read-through. Phillips hopes that as she reads, something unpredictable will occur to her. She said, "I need to have an idea of what I'd do if I were directing it. This movie or play is about this . . . this is the theme . . . what are the big archetypes, the metaphors, here?" She is determined to get the big picture before she thinks about her role. Once she's done five read-throughs, she studies her character's key, transitional scene. After that, it's easier to understand the end and the beginning for her character.

Los Angeles actor Leo Marks has devised his own way of approaching the text for the first time. He starts off by trying to find what's strange in the script. That's how he shakes himself out of complacency, out of a tendency to make assumptions. He asks himself, Why is this happening this way and not some other way? What are the alternative possibilities? In this scene, what are the other things that could happen? Why am I silent right here? What are the things that would make sense for me to say that I'm *not* saying?

So he's looking at the script from his own character's viewpoint, rather than more directorially, as Phillips does, and seeking a world of possibilities and subtext. "I begin the work of finding the kind of spontaneity you're always looking for by shaking off the curse of knowing what's going to happen next," he said.

He also separates the givens from the non-givens. For example, if the character is from Northumberland, an accent is a given. Maybe a limp is a given, and something he can start working on. "All the things you're relatively certain of, you want to become fluent with, so you can then give in to the uncertain."

Another actor told me he usually reads a play two to three times before the first rehearsal. At least one of those is just for the story, another to look at specific interactions among characters. He also looks for the changes his own character goes through, his character's consistency and inconsistency. And he looks at the stage directions, but never first, and only as a springboard for possibilities, not as a guideline. Some actors scratch out the stage directions immediately. He sometimes reads his lines aloud, but only just before the first rehearsal, to make sure the words come out of his mouth right. He thinks reading aloud is a bad idea because it becomes about what can-I-do-with-that-line rather than about the story.

For Marks, it's dangerous to get too methodical about any part of the process, so he has no set number of times he reads the script. And he's more concerned with interrogating particular pieces of the play, engaging with them, rather than just reading from start to finish. A dense play could require many readings, perhaps daily. He likes to laugh as he reads, find out what's delightful about it. Also, he likes to walk in strange neighborhoods with his script—"something about the unfamiliar homes passing before my eyes shakes it up nicely for me," he said.

In *Directing Actors,* Judith Weston poses these questions: What is the play's main, and deepest, conflict? Who is the antagonist, who the protagonist? What is the main action? Ultimately, what is the play's theme—what is the author trying to say about the human condition?

Let's go back to the specifics of Shelton's process. In one sentence, say *what the play is about.* If the playwright is good—and for the purposes of this discussion, let's assume that to be so—the theme is universal. That doesn't mean we all need to agree on what the theme is; it can be a subjective thing. We used Sam Shepard's *True West* as our first exercise in class, so I'll use it here. I think *True West* is about sibling rivalry. *You* may think *True West* is about finding one's own identity, or about failure, or something else entirely.

Next, *examine each scene* individually. What is it about, what is its function in the play? This too can be subjective. Shelton thinks that the first scene in *True West* is about the two brothers reaching out to each other and missing. I'm not so sure. I think it may be about each marking his own territory. What do you think?

Now it's time to examine the script from your own character's POV. First, what are the *given circumstances*—that is, why is your character here and what baggage has he brought with him? The script will provide most of the answers; the rest you'll have to fill in. Which means that every actor who is preparing to play, for example, the role of Lee, the rough brother in *True West,* will have a slightly different, individually tailored, set of given circumstances. Shelton cautioned against writing a lengthy biography of your character. Choose only those circumstances that will help you play the scene.

In our classroom exercise, we examined the character of Lee. Shelton started out by mulling over the first few lines of the play. She recalled everything she knew about Lee from reading the entire play, in order to create given circumstances for Lee that would work for her were she playing the role:

Lee: So, Mom took off for Alaska, huh?
Austin: Yeah.
Lee: Sorta left you in charge.

Lee has arrived from his isolated desert home thinking he'd see his mother, but instead he finds his screenwriter brother, Austin, who has been given temporary custody of the house. Lee hasn't seen Austin in years. Their father also lives in the desert, and he's sick, so something has to be done. Lee has no money. Is he here to get money? To find help for his father?

Knowing, and making decisions about, the given circumstances lead naturally to *adjustments.* Adjustments are not your character's feelings per se but rather your character's point of view at any given moment—particularly his point of view upon entering the scene, or upon a major change of beat (see below for discussion of beats). The clue to your adjustment, once again, is within the play itself. What is Lee's adjustment when he says his first line? For Jean Shelton, it's *cautious:* He wasn't expecting to find Austin there and he's not sure how he feels about it. If I were playing Lee, I think I'd choose *hostile.* I think Lee knows exactly how he feels about Austin in this situation.

Next you want to look for *beats,* the chunks of text of which the scene is composed. When the subject of the dialogue or the action clearly changes, that's when a new beat begins. You'll want to understand exactly what your character is doing within each beat. You might be: 1) wanting something from the other character(s); 2) engaged in a personal physical task; or 3) sharing a story or memory. One of these three activities will be your character's primary—although not sole—point of concentration.

Now it's time to *personalize.* "You must always be present and find a way that you can personally relate to your character," said Shelton. "Take the situation of the character and create a detailed memory/reality to use as truthful reference for the lines in the scene." Make all your choices as personally meaningful yet as close to the reality of the play as possible.

If I were playing Lee in *True West,* I would feel that Lee is jealous of Austin for many specific reasons. I have a sister. I know all about jealousy and sibling rivalry, and I bet you do, too. If you can effectively personalize, you will naturally care about what you are doing, and you'll be at one with your character, so you won't have to work for the emotion.

You must also look for ways to *physicalize,* said Shelton. Physicalizing helps get you out of your head and into your body. "The more you can physicalize anything onstage, the more of an impact you make," she noted.

As you follow this analysis process for every line and beat and scene of the play, your character will emerge bit by bit, evolving as the play develops, like a Polaroid snapshot.

The key when analyzing is to go from the general to the specific: from an understanding of what the play is about to an understanding of what each scene is about to what you personally know about it all, on a moment to moment, beat by beat, action by action level.

As you examine your script, always seek to *empathize* with your character. To hone your empathy skills, Shelton suggests observing others and trying to understand their motives and their emotions. Why is empathy so important? If you can't empathize with your character, whether it be Iago in *Othello* or Amanda in *The Glass Menagerie* or Adolph Hitler, you will be playing one-dimensionally. Let the audience judge whether your character is good or evil (for more on playing meanies, see Chapter 9, "Touch of Evil: Playing Villains"). Your job is to work with the playwright's words to motivate, defend, and support your character.

Ultimately, the method you choose to tackle the script will be your own. Uta Hagen in *A Challenge to the Actor* advises approaching the task with an innocent, wide-open mind, but without overintellectualizing—it's the director's job to do a complete analysis of the script, she says, but you want to arrive at the first rehearsal as a creative participant, not as an übermarionette. Why? Because a thoughtful, well-prepared actor with a mind of his or her own commands—or should command—a certain respect.

Chapter 27

MEMORIZATION

I've heard it said that Charlie Chaplin quit acting when it got too hard to memorize lines. You'd think that the more you practice a technique, the easier it becomes. But for most of us, as we age, our memories deteriorate. Memorization—once the least of our problems when approaching a new role—is increasingly a challenge, even for those of us who always considered ourselves quick studies.

There are many tricks and methods for prodding a recalcitrant memory. Here's one taught in Los Angeles by Vicki Mizel. It involves substituting visual images for key words in your script, then mentally linking up the images—in fact, activating them in your mind's eye—in proper sequence. With a lot of practice, the method apparently works. Mizel has been teaching it for years (to Alzheimer's patients and others, as well as to actors), and I talked to a few actors who have had success with it and say it's also lots of fun.

Let's take a specific short monologue, the servant Luka's speech from the beginning of *The Brute,* a one-act play by Anton Chekhov. The lines are,

"It's not right, ma'am, you're killing yourself. The cook has gone off with the maid to pick berries. The cat is having a high old time in the yard catching birds. Every living thing is happy, but you stay moping here in the house like it was a convent, taking no pleasure in nothing. I mean it, ma'am, it must be a full year since you set foot out of doors."

Step 1. For each line or section of a line, choose a key word or phrase. I chose *not right* for the first half of the first line, *killing yourself* for the second half.

Step 2. Then choose a concrete visual image for both key words. Anything will do if it works for you, although the closer you can stick to the script's meaning, the better. I chose an image of myself with my sweater on inside out (*not right*), followed by a woman stabbing herself with a knife (*killing yourself*). Mizel says it's important to start off with an image of yourself or the character, then dispense with that human image and proceed.

Step 3. In your mind's eye, place the first image (inverted sweater) on the left, and place the second image (suicidal woman) on the right.

Step 4. Then link up the two images so that the image on the left is doing something physically interactive with the image on the right. Choose an active verb with an "ing" ending, such as *squeezing, hugging, cuddling, eating.* Avoid non-active verbs like *seeing, hearing, watching.* Remember, it doesn't have to make sense, but if you can choose a verb that's close to the action described in the text, so much the better. I imagined the sweater *tugging* the knife from the suicidal woman's hand. Goofy, seemingly irrelevant, but hard to forget.

See where this process is going? Images are easier to remember than individual words; active images are easier to remember than static ones; and it's natural to remember images from left to right because that's the way we read in English. Also, says Mizel, small things tend to remind you of the large.

You can continue with Luka's monologue yourself, by writing down a key word for each group of words, drawing a symbol for your key word, then activating and linking up those images in your mind's eye. For example, I chose an apron for the *cook,* a frilly cap for the *maid,* and a blackberry bush for *berries.* For the first pair of images, the apron's sash might be *slapping* the frilly cap. For the second pair, the cap might be *impaling* itself upon the blackberry brambles.

It's important to see the visual images in as much detail as possible; to concentrate on only two images at a time in order to keep the sequence straight (the image on the left disappears, the image on the right moves to the left, a new image appears on the right); and to keep your eyes open while visualizing. Mizel's instructional tape suggests imagining you're looking through the lens of a camera or a telescope. The more of your senses you can involve, the better for your memory retention—and the better for your acting in general, of course. If you're visualizing an orange, smell it and taste it.

What about words in the script that are less tangible than *cook* or *maid*? For those, you need the sounds-like method. Say you need to remember the word *tangible.* Well, turn *tangible* into *tangerine,* a concrete thing that you can also smell and taste and touch.

Once you've visualized your images and the active sequential associations for them, it's time to test your recall. Mizel suggests that you jog your memory by asking it questions. So, going back to our Luka speech, we'd start out by asking, "What is the person on the left doing?" The answer is, she's got her sweater on backwards, which means something is wrong ("It's not right, ma'am") and she's tugging at the knife of a woman who's stabbing herself ("you're killing yourself").

In the beginning, it's important to follow the word-symbol exercise, cautions Mizel: key word/phrase; symbol; action verb; link them up. Once you're adept at the technique, you can take short cuts; Mizel draws a little picture above words in her script, then writes down an action in the margin.

Mizel notes that you should not expect this method to work instantly, and in fact, since the exercises discussed here are fairly advanced, you'll probably need a basic grounding in the system (you can order her tapes at brain-sproutsmemory.com). It takes lots of practice and, in the beginning, as much time as rote memorization. But the more you use your visual ability, the more powerful it becomes, and images start flowing in. Not only do these images stay locked in your long-term memory for easy recall, but the work of developing them strengthens your actorly skills, including sense memory, imagination, and general creativity.

Mizel suggests that during the first week of learning this method, you should make a list of seven to ten items and memorize them every day. During the next week, practice the sounds-like method. Then, finally, proceed to work on a script.

"Most of the time we can't learn lines because it's not interesting to us," said Diane Salinger, another Los Angeles teacher, who took Mizel's class. "And there are certain scripts," she added, "that are not well written and it's not interesting to the mind, and that's when you have the most trouble. So when you can actually spark real interest and make it creative, then the mind is interested."

She chooses cartoon-like images and has fun animating them as she links them.

I asked both her and Mizel if working so hard to develop these images during the memorization process can interfere when you're actually acting. "By the time you're onstage you know this stuff so well that a sunflower, say, will just be a fleeting image, and you'll be in the scene," Mizel assured me.

"The images can actually help your acting," elaborated Salinger, who encourages her students to choose images related to their objective. In any case, they won't hurt. Just as in real life you're seeing a variety of images when you're talking to someone—the party he's describing, the sandwich you're about to eat, the pimple on his nose, a fly buzzing around, the broccoli that might be stuck between your teeth—so those fleeting images that you may retain from your memorization process shouldn't interfere with what's happening on stage or on camera.

Professional opera singer turned actor Teryl Warren finds that the sequencing aspect of Mizel's memorization method is especially helpful when faced with scripts that lack logical transitions. Making transitions believable is the actor's job, but it's especially hard to memorize a script that jumps around. However, said Warren, with this method, "You can always go from the previous thought to the next thought" by visualizing those linked actions.

He'd only been using the method for three months when I talked to him but said that for him it's faster than rote memorization, although it does take time to come up with the images. He said he has latched onto certain images that he re-uses. For example, to remember the word *everything,* he visualizes the hand of Thing from *The Munsters,* and imagines the hand gathering up Eveready batteries. Sounds convoluted, but it's fun, and Warren says it works.

For German-born actor Marcus Jung, the images help him to be in what he calls the more creative side of his mind. Previously he'd always found himself mired in memorizing instead of working on the acting. Now he feels self-confident enough to work on the acting first and the memorization later, which he finds highly preferable.

"If you have a fear of learning lines, do something about it before you need to, so you have a technique down already," advised Salinger.

Is it necessary to take a class to learn this approach? Jung, who took Mizel's class at the Learning Annex, thinks it would be just as hard to learn this method from a tape as to learn how to act from a tape, and prefers the classroom setting. Warren found that one tutorial did the trick. "You basically teach this to yourself," he said. "No one can do the images for you. But you do need self-discipline."

For other useful approaches I talked to actors in their fifties, sixties, and seventies, the time when most people start to experience mild memory loss. They all had ways of coping. Mix and match as you will. The more of your five senses you can involve, the better, advised one actor.

- Let your body remember. Even if you haven't ridden a bicycle in years, you don't have to think about how to do it; you just climb on and trust your muscles to do the rest. If you create associations between the text and your body, your movement can actually activate your speech.

   An actor in his 80s tries to find some stage business to associate with the lines. He says it doesn't matter if there's no obvious connection between the words and your action. Try setting up your living room to resemble the set and move around it as you're doing lines. Another, who memorized a two-hour monologue, Chaucer's "The Knight's Tale," expressed it this way: "Get it into the body. Move with the words."

   A director who'd once worked with Laurence Olivier told an actor that one of the methods Olivier used was to "teach the lines to your mouth." The actor explained it to me via e-mail: "Olivier would take the time to repeat the lines very slowly using the mouth and tongue muscles in a very exaggerated way. I've always found that using this 'muscular memory' in the early stages of learning lines is much more reliable than trying to psychologically 'remember' the lines—and more true to life, since most people don't 'think' about what they're saying, they spontaneously talk. Once the lines become second nature to your muscles, then you can think about what you should be thinking about onstage—i.e., your objectives."

- Visualize. Many actors picture the position of their lines on the page. This helps them figure out what comes next. By the time the show has been running for awhile, that visual memory usually fades. Other actors find that typing out their lines helps to imprint them on the memory. One actor writes all his cues and lines out by hand several times over.

- Use your auditory memory. On an Internet website, one actor wrote, "I think it's important to discover for yourself whether you are a person who learns best by hearing or seeing. I struggled for a while until I eventually realized I was learning the other characters' lines faster than I was learning my own. And I guessed that maybe the reason was that I was hearing their lines at rehearsal while I was only seeing mine. I persuaded friends to read my lines to me."

  And tape recorders can be a useful tool. One actor reads the entire play into a cassette and then plays the tape back over and over, saying his own lines in unison. Another, who has performed a number of solo pieces, puts her own lines on tape (and, if there are other characters, she adds their cue lines). Yet another tapes only the other actor's lines.

  Try listening to music while you're memorizing. "If I can find the right piece of music—classical, but not necessarily—that has a feel of the piece, it helps," reported an actor who works along with the sound, relating the words to it in whatever way he can. "It's another hook to pull me along. The more hooks you can find, intellectually, physically in terms of your location on the stage, the better." An added benefit is that listening to complex music is believed by researchers to exercise the brain, thereby potentially strengthening memory.

- Physicalize. Lots of actors find they're more mentally alert moving while they memorize. One walks around a playing field, script in hand, at least an hour a day before and during the rehearsal period and during performance. I saw another, plodding through a neighborhood park, with cigar and script, mumbling to himself—three days a week, along with his co-actor, for the month before he started rehearsing *Waiting for Godot*.

  In Alzheimer's studies, researchers have found that increased blood flow during physical exercise sends more oxygen and nutrients to the brain and can in fact help memory.

- Eat right. An actor told me he'd received fourteen days' notice to fill in as the lead in *The Guardsman.* "The role is bigger than God," he said. "Normally for me a good deal of memorization happens during rehearsal, but there simply wasn't time for this." He popped vitamins and gingko biloba (which some scientists recommend to aid memory); "I swear by the stuff," he said. "I think it helps my mental alertness."

- Know your objectives. A rule of Method acting, this technique shouldn't be ignored as an aid to memorization. If you can, break the script down into beats before you start to memorize, and have a clear idea of what your character wants during each beat.

Finally, relax. Although it may take you longer to learn lines as you age, you'll probably retain them just as well.

Chapter 28

SHOOTING OUT
OF SEQUENCE

How do you create a fluid, organic arc for your character when shooting a film out of sequence—which is almost always the case?

Veteran Los Angeles actor Stephen Tobolowsky, who has appeared in (to name only a few) *Groundhog Day, The Grifters,* and *Burn Hollywood Burn: An Alan Smithee Film,* once had to shoot an out-of-sequence phone conversation with actor Trey Wilson for *Great Balls of Fire.* Wilson filmed his half of the conversation on location in Memphis. Then the cast moved to London, where Tobolowsky shot his half. But in the intervening month Wilson had died. "It was emotional for me and the cast not only to lose such a person but then to have to play a scene with him when he'd died a week before in the United States," said Tobolowsky.

At other times, he's had to shoot the last scene at the beginning and much later on shoot the scene that immediately precedes it. But anything can happen in between: the director may have changed his or her mind, and now the tone of the preceding scene is different. Sometimes there will be reshooting, sometimes not.

But Tobolowsky is pragmatic and in fact adjusted my perspective considerably. "In television and film," he explained, "you're talking about bigger challenges to the actor's craft than shooting out of sequence." He ticked off a few: lengthy setups; hours of makeup followed by thirty seconds of acting, followed by more makeup; scenes shot backward, forward, any which way; lack of rehearsals; last-minute changes in the context of the scene.

Still, let's stick with the topic at hand. Some of the many reasons for shooting out of sequence (as outlined in Steve Carlson's book, *Hitting Your Mark*): 1) If scenes in different parts of the film take place in the same location, naturally all those scenes will be shot consecutively; 2) sunlight, shadow, rain, etc. (including seasonal changes) affect the sequence of a shoot; and 3) changes in actors' personal appearance, and the length of their individual contracts, are other factors.

Tobolowsky noted one more: the possibility of an actor's death before the film wraps. In *Bird on a Wire* with Mel Gibson, he said, the director shot Tobolowsky's scenes but saved for last the scene in which he was to fall forty feet into a tank of piranhas with forty pounds of lead in his pocket to hold him there. That way, in case he was eaten by a piranha, his scenes would already be in the can. (On the other hand, the late Oliver Reed was digitally resuscitated to complete *Gladiator,* the film during which he inconveniently died. And in the scenario presented by the 2002 Al Pacino film *Simone,* a digital actor replaced one who'd walked off the shoot. But we're digressing here.)

In Tobolowsky's experience, gifted directors often start by shooting unchallenging scenes: getting in and out of a car, going upstairs, listening in on a phone conversation—the nuts and bolts stuff. Then, a week or two or three later, when camaraderie and chemistry have been established, the director schedules the big scenes that are not carried by special effects.

"Non-gifted directors don't care," asserted Tobolowsky. "Your first day in the morning you may have to do a big climax, the culmination of your entire part, before you know anyone."

Yet Tobolowsky insists that shooting out of sequence is a day at the beach compared to—for example—reacting to things that aren't there. "In *The Philadelphia Experiment,* they told me to react to a special effect, a big vortex," he said. "I asked, 'What does it look like?' They said, 'We don't know yet.' . . . Basically, a [film] actor's performance is cobbled together. That just comes to the amount of preparation you do before film starts."

So: How do you prepare for shooting topsy-turvy, bass ackwards, and inside out, not to mention all the other distracting elements of film making?

Tobolowsky looks at the whole movie and asks himself what the central idea is, in one sentence. "Don't intellectualize," he cautioned. "Just one sentence. *Sixth Sense,* for example, is about courage. That's the spine. Regardless of what your role is, you have to understand your part in telling that story. Are you an item of fear? Do you lead to the development of courage or do you impede it? Are you a heartening or discouraging factor? Then you say to yourself, What is the essence of each of my scenes? I may not [appear in] the essential moment of the scene, but I have to identify it and know how I contribute to it. Once I know that, I don't have to intellectualize the entire process of where I am when I am. I understand the stakes, what the scene is about, and how I contribute."

And when you arrive on the set? "You just let it happen," said Tobolowsky. "You even surprise yourself. . . . You just go there knowing what you know, not having worked out everything. After all, you don't know where the camera will be, or what the other actor will bring. . . . You might rehearse the scene like two normal people. Then they set up the cameras. Then they say 'OK, just a couple of things. The person you're talking to instead of standing up is on a pile of sandbags. And you come in walking bowlegged and shoeless so you'll match his height. We'll shoot you from the waist up.' And you do it trying not to laugh, pretending you're two guys just standing and talking. The movie business is full of people saying lean left, lean right. Plenty of things stand in the way of you and your performance. The only way to get around that is to understand the elements of the story and how you play into that."

Laura Henry, who teaches Meisner, Alexander, and audition techniques in Los Angeles, believes that understanding the arc of your role and being good at script analysis are crucial skills in film acting. "Jimmy Stewart was great at that," she told me. "When you watch his films you can't tell which scene was shot first. With beginning actors you can sometimes tell." You could actually use a number system ("I need a #20 preparation here") to organize the emotional moments in the script and chart the ebb and flow of real time, she said, although she doesn't necessarily recommend that technique.

"You're basically dealing with how your relationships with the other characters have changed, what your circumstances are, how all that relates to the rest of the script," she continued. She agreed with Tobolowsky that what you do on a set "isn't about regular acting. You might be reading with the first a.d. and you have to hurry up because you're losing the light or the weather. . . . In theatre if you get the beginning well and you've done your homework, it all goes moment to moment and adds up. But in film you have to create that piecemeal."

She also pointed out that you have to be able to do an emotional preparation forty times instead of once. "In film you do your homework at home by yourself, which is a difficult way to work. And you have to bring it in and be specific and full on the first take and on the fortieth take. Stewart, De Niro, Streep, Kevin Spacey—they make emotional sense every time."

I asked Tobolowsky if he'd ever shot a film in sequence. Yes, he said, but "it isn't like you do it in one day. It may be over the course of two months. You shoot a scene, go home, eat a meal, come back the next day. The only advantage of in-sequence is onstage, where you gain momentum by doing it in front of an audience. In a film first they shoot the master, which they may never use. Then a two-shot, then another close-up, an insert, another insert, a high angle. You end up shooting bits and pieces anyway.

"The biggest problem is not the sequence issue," he reiterated, "but being able to go to zero. [For example,] in the movie *Hero,* director Stephen Frears shot sixty-seven takes of one scene. He may have used take thirty-five or take sixty-seven, but he probably didn't use number one. A lot of times you've been affected by all the previous takes. Whether the start of the scene is high or neutral, after several takes it's hard to get back to that starting point, wherever it is. You have to find that way of starting the scene at the right place, at ground zero." Tobolowsky observed that the tip of Diane Keaton's nose always gets red in emotional scenes. If she starts a scene with a red nose (from a previous take), an astute viewer knows that an intense moment is imminent. Gifted as she is, she can hardly control her autonomic nervous system!

What advice would you give to a first-time film actor who's used to doing stage? I asked Tobolowsky.

"Learn your part well but not your line readings," he said promptly. "A lot of times when actors work on their lines without the benefit of rehearsal, they practice and come up with clever line readings. That stuff doesn't work. You're on the set and they're running out of time and they say, 'Instead of doing a lot of setups and having this scene take place in an office, let's just have you running down the hall.'" In *Groundhog Day,* Harold Ramis wasn't sure he wanted the day itself to be in sunlight, shade, or snow, so the actors had to be prepared to go in different directions. "Learn your part but not your line readings," said Tobolowsky. That advice doesn't specifically relate to shooting out of sequence, but it's good advice for acting in general.

"Film and TV is about being thrown," he added. "If you can make the wildness of the environment your ally, it's going to make whatever you do spontaneous and fresh."

Chapter 29

HERE WE GO
LOOP-DE-LOOP: LOOPING

When you're called back into the studio after you've shot your scene(s), to re-record your dialogue, one line at a time—that's looping. This is a common occurrence in film, and almost as common in TV, according to Los Angeles TV and film veteran Steve Carlson (whose book *Hitting Your Mark* is a nuts-and-bolts guide for those just starting out in media work). Looping is necessary for the obvious reason that during the shoot ambient noise may interfere with the clarity of the dialogue, or with continuity. An exception might be if the film has been shot on a sound stage.

As Carlson explains in his book, looping is done in a special audio studio. You'll probably be standing, with earphones on, in a dark room with a large screen on one wall. For film, when you're thirty feet tall, it's important to lip synch very precisely. You'll be flying solo. Through the earphones you'll hear a series of three beeps. This creates a rhythm that you'll want to learn how to groove to—your dialogue starts exactly at the fourth beep. So take your breath just ahead of that. "The picture . . . starts about ten seconds or so before the line to be recorded comes up," writes Carlson. He adds that often there's a white line that creeps from the right side of the screen. "This line will move across the screen to the left, hitting the end of the screen at the exact moment you should begin your dialogue. . . . the pulse of the beeps will also lead you to that split second." In a phone conversation Carlson added that if you have any kind of musical ability, that will help you, since so much of the skill involves rhythm.

The question is, assuming you quickly get the hang of matching your words to the onscreen image, how do you re-create the feeling that you worked so hard to nail when you originally shot the scene?

"We've all seen bad looping—technically the actor's voice may be in synch but somehow the feeling is slightly off," I said. "Why?"

117

"It's hard many times to get back the same emotional involvement," Carlson acknowledged. "People who are good at looping are very animated when they do it. They're all over the place doing silly, crazy things. They talk big with their hands. They run. They jump. You've got to have a scowl, stomp around, get physical. You do as much as you can to bring back the feeling of whatever you were doing on camera. The same with a love scene. It's not just the technique of matching the voice; you have to match the emotion."

How, exactly? No doubt here's where all your sense memory works comes in handy, to conjure up that magical moment when you shot that scene—greatly aided, of course, by the picture on the screen right in front of you. Carlson said that if you've spent enough time with your character to know the character's "colors," it's not all that hard to look at the screen and re-imagine for yourself the emotional circumstances that existed when those lines were filmed. How long ago would that have been? Probably two to four weeks for TV, said Carlson, and maybe as long as two or three months for film, although he guessed a month might be an average for film.

So, is looping scary or fun? Fun, asserted Carlson. More importantly, it's an opportunity to fine-tune your performance. "You can do something as small as put a little more smile in your voice," he suggested. When you paste a smile on your face and talk through it, he pointed out, the listener can hear the difference; you sound brighter. But on camera you couldn't necessarily do that; it could look silly. Or during looping you might, for example, realize you didn't talk loud enough to appear realistic in a busy outdoor scene, so now's your chance to belt it a little more. When looked at from the perspective of having a chance to improve your performance, looping becomes a less intimidating proposition for the beginner.

What should you avoid doing? Don't try to change anything too much, cautioned Carlson. You basically want to duplicate the performance you've got up there. Subtle shading and coloring is as far as you can go. "If you think you can change the actual reading, even if you get the timing right, that won't work," he explained, "because there's another actor responding to you, and if you said your line differently, their response would have been different." Too true.

Can you prepare for a looping session? No, because you don't know what scenes or lines you'll be doing. "So don't get into a dither," advised Carlson. "These guys [the technicians] who do looping, they're specialists. Most of the time they're working with actors who don't really know what they're doing. It's a no-pressure situation." The looping technicians, he assured me, will help the novice actor.

Is it weird and otherworldly, seeing yourself up there and having to re-create a past experience? I wondered. After all, this will be the first time you see yourself onscreen in that particular role.

"It is kind of weird," Carlson agreed. In TV looping, he noted, you may be in a small booth, and you may see yourself on a TV monitor. Or not even that: You may just hear yourself in the earphones.

For their part, the technicians are looking for clean dialogue. As Carlson explained, most of the time in natural conversation, dialogue overlaps. In order for the sound technicians to manipulate dialogue, they first need it synched and clean. Even your "oh yeahs" need to be pristine and clear. Then the sound designers may bunch them up, or slide the dialogue around digitally in any manner of ways. "If you're a quarter of a second slow with your lip synch but they like the reading, they'll stretch the line a quarter of a second and it won't change the pitch of the voice or anything," he said.

I wondered if a good actor can through no fault of his/her own be a bad looper. "I worked with an actor in westerns at Universal," Carlson recalled. "He was the worst looper in the world—he hated it. He couldn't help it. Yes, you can still be a good actor and not be a natural at looping. So you may have to work a little harder." Carlson himself, so confident at looping, once auditioned to dub into English the voice of an actor in an Italian film. He quickly discovered that looping and dubbing, which seem so similar, are two separate skills. He didn't get the job.

Consider looping a new experience, he suggested—one that will give you a chance to do that scene again . . . and better.

Chapter 30

SEXUAL NUDITY

Some actors wouldn't accept a role that includes sexual nudity; others might eagerly take up the challenge. Most of us would weigh the pros and cons, and, if we go ahead with the job, approach it with some trepidation.

At age thirty-two, Flynn De Marco never imagined he'd appear nude onstage. So when he replaced a member of the cast in *10 Naked Men* at San Francisco's Theatre Rhinoceros, and had to go on stark naked, he was absolutely terrified. Freaking out in the wings, he had to be literally shoved onstage the first night. But he followed that with a role as a gay teenage junkie hustler in *Shopping and Fucking*, a sexually graphic drama by British writer Mark Ravenhill. How sexually graphic? Enough to make the audience queasy. In one scene De Marco was inches away from and facing the audience, leaning forward over the back of a couch, being (ahem) f***ed from behind. In another, he was downstage center being raped by two mates, and he was required to be extremely emotionally involved, to put it delicately. Both scenes were staged pants-down for all the actors.

"I was really nervous before the dress rehearsal," he confided. The dress rehearsal was the first time the cast appeared in the almost-altogether. It helped that the director reminded the cast, "These scenes are about sex, not about seeing your willy." (The gritty *Shopping* presents sexuality as a marketable commodity in a spiritually bankrupt and commercialized society.) Plus, said De Marco, it helped that the director downplayed the whole issue, didn't foster a lot of anxiety and suspense around it.

The next big hurdle for De Marco was the opening. "My stomach was a mess, I had butterflies," he said. Luckily, he was blindfolded in the rape scene and didn't have to be distracted by seeing the audience.

The key to accepting the nudity and difficult material was, for De Marco, feeling comfortable with the cast. The first time they blocked the violent rape scene, all the actors were in tears. "I was upset from crying and screaming, the others were afraid of hurting me. It was scary," said De Marco.

"Afterward we sat around and hugged. . . . We had to trust each other and get really close during rehearsals. We hung out a lot together. And all of us are very physical people, so coming into rehearsals there were always big, long hugs and cuddling, so that helped." Once the trust was established, De Marco was able to focus on developing his character, Gary. "I know Gary," he said. "If it hadn't been for lucky circumstances, I could have been him, that's sort of how I look at it."

Valerie Dillman, who played the eponymous, sexually free Lulu in German playwright Frank Wedekind's drama, agreed that trust is an important issue when taking on overtly sexual roles. At the very end of the play, she was completely nude, being murdered by Jack the Ripper. Throughout, she was scantily clad (one outfit was essentially a butt-thong) and seductive; she had to kiss every male in the cast, from a fourteen-year-old boy to much older men, plus a lesbian character. A member of Los Angeles' Pacific Resident Theatre, she knew her co-actors, and isn't sure she would have done the play with complete strangers. Plus, the director had the cast do trust exercises and play silly games at the beginning to get comfortable with the delicate material.

Unlike De Marco, Dillman had no fears about nudity; she describes herself as not very modest. And, used to playing good-girl roles and considering herself unskilled at the female art of attracting men to her, she was eager to explore her own sexuality through Lulu, a promiscuous "kept woman" and sexual magnet for both males and females. How did she go about it?

For her, the key was to avoid a general, clichéd idea of sexuality, or other people's notions about it. "I tried to get in touch with what made me feel sexy," said Dillman. "Even if it's just putting on a big T-shirt. I went to Victoria's Secret. I read all of Anaïs Nin's diaries and some Jeanette Winterson. I wanted to become more aware of what made me personally feel sexy."

Once she'd gotten in touch with that side of herself, she realized that for Lulu, she needed to focus not on her own sexuality but on arousing others. Fully committing herself to that objective freed her from self-consciousness. She had to come up with inventive ways to turn the other characters on, whether by explicit and physically aggressive actions or by more subtle means. "That became journal work," she said, "thinking about the different people, what might turn them on." The real people? "Yes, you have to use the real people, as they present themselves through their characters. What gets people going in general, what in specific?" As a woman, she found it easier to do that with the female character: "I had a better idea of what works with a woman."

De Marco and Dillman both said it made no difference whether the sex-and-nudity scene was with a male or female. It basically just comes down to identifying with your character and playing your objective, just as you would do in any other type of scene.

Although Dillman spent a lot of time working on ways of being seductive that didn't necessarily rely on bodily contact, there was plenty of touching, too—French kissing, crotch-grabbing. She varied her activities from night to night to get the desired effect from the other characters. Was it initially hard to grab a man's crotch, put his hand up her shirt? No. Her concentration was on accomplishing her goals as Lulu.

As for the nudity, that was not rehearsed at all. "You wear things to make you feel sexy and then when it's just your body, you don't feel very sexy. You notice your flaws more," said Dillman. "With clothes you can cover things up and accentuate them, but when you're naked it's different. I didn't want to *not* do it out of vanity. The night before the preview I tossed and turned—will I look like a dork? But I wanted to see the effect. So I did it. It was fine, it was kind of freeing. Just me, naked, my body, that's it. It got me to a place of acceptance. The director said that at the end I seemed pathetic, like a little girl, and I liked the idea of that stripped-down effect, that Lulu was this little girl who just wanted love."

Things to watch out for when playing roles of this nature? Dillman got a 6 a.m. phone call after opening night from someone claiming to be a producer. "I was a little bit scared, I thought maybe I've opened up Pandora's box, I put this out there and there was something dark about it that I'd never thought of before," she said. Fortunately, nothing bad happened.

"I don't think I would want to do anything where I was fully naked onstage for a really long time," mused De Marco. During early rehearsals for *Shopping,* he was quite uneasy anticipating the nudity, but he lost fifteen pounds during rehearsals (partly to play a character half his age) and felt better by opening. For actors who are planning to appear nude, he recommended walking around the house buck naked just to get comfortable with the feeling. "And also I think you might want to consider why the nudity is there," he said. "Decide how you feel about being objectified for your nudity, just to sell tickets, as opposed to the nudity being there to move the plot."

Challenging as the nudity-sexuality combo was for both these actors, neither regrets it for a minute. "Doing this show has helped me grow as an actor," said De Marco. "Getting those things out on stage is almost like a weird sort of therapy, to get that raw with people, and to know they're not going to freak out on you."

On stage or screen, sexual nudity is commonplace these days, and I don't think it's going to disappear anytime soon. I agree with De Marco and Dillman that roles like these, which challenge you to face your fears, overcome your vanity, and reveal scary sides of yourself, can be quite liberating. Just make sure trust is established first.

Chapter 31

ACTING WITH THE ENEMY

An acting teacher (let's call him "Constantin") once told me that one of his students, let's call her "Tallulah," did not want to work on a scene with her assigned partner—er, "Marlon." She said that Marlon made her uncomfortable, but she was unable (or unwilling) to elaborate further. When Constantin told Marlon that he'd be reassigned, Marlon was distressed. He didn't understand Tallulah's unwillingness to work with him (she hadn't talked to him directly). Because of lack of specific information, Constantin had no idea whether sexual harassment or cultural miscommunication were involved (Marlon and Tallulah were of two different cultures).

In this case, the problem was easy to fix: reassign partners. But what if you're in a play or film—maybe even a long-running tour or TV series—and you just can't stand someone in the cast?

Some people have the gift of being able to separate their stage persona from their—well, personal persona. Years ago in summer stock, one actor not only had to act with a lead whom the entire company disliked, he also self-lessly volunteered to room with the creep. "I still remember the smell of the cologne he wore," shuddered the martyr. "I hated that smell." Nevertheless, "As long as he could do the job in a somewhat professional manner, I could separate my personal feelings." More recently, he acted with a woman whom he didn't particularly like, "but I thought her work onstage was brilliant, so anything else didn't matter." In fact, he said, "I'd rather work with someone who I don't like offstage but can trust onstage rather than the reverse, if I had to choose. You're too vulnerable out there." He's been onstage with likable co-actors who just weren't up to the mark professionally. "I try not to deal with people I don't like offstage. But when we're at work, we're at work."

Another veteran actor agreed: He mentioned a "chilly" relationship with a costar, but "I concentrated on the immediate task and put aside personal feelings. If the other person is hitting their marks and playing ball, things can go smoothly [onstage]."

Others, though, have had to struggle to keep their offstage feelings from contaminating their work. An actor recalled a traumatic incident in which her co-actor, with whom she hadn't been communicating well, switched her objective for a particular scene immediately before the first performance without sharing that plan in advance, and it changed the whole scene. Some actors might relish the challenge of facing something new, but not this person. "When we got to that scene," she said, "I got so wrapped up in how outrageous this was that it destroyed my performance. . . . I wasn't a big enough actor or person to truly let it go." Now, she makes a habit of meditating before rehearsal and performance. "I think that anger comes from your own anxiety," she said. "It was a big warning sign to me about how that can affect your work. I knew after it was all over that it was as much about me as about the other actor. I don't know if the meditation has mellowed me out, but I just don't seem to run into those kinds of situations."

Maura Vincent, an actor/teacher in Los Angeles, also had to face her own anxieties. "I was on the road for a year with an actor where we were both leads and couldn't stand each other," she said. "I kept saying it was his problem. After the tour I did some rethinking and realized there was a pattern to my own work that had to do with vulnerability. . . . I hadn't done enough exploration of my own blocks. I had projected it onto this person so as to relieve culpability for my own success or failure."

Psychotherapy can help you confront those kinds of problems. On an immediate level, though, how do you prevent pesky negative feelings from interfering with your performance?

A show biz veteran who'd worked with both Zero Mostel and Milton Berle found them both to be downright obnoxious prima donnas. "You have to find a way to use it," she said. In one case, she let the situation make her character more depressed.

But in many cases you're required to actually love the person you loathe. One woman developed an antipathy to the man she was playing opposite when he kept slightly injuring her in a fight scene. Yet he played her husband and they also had to cuddle. She relied on the old actor's trick of isolating the positive qualities of the other person. "I tried to look at him as a specimen," she said. "OK, he has nice legs. I like his ears. Finding those things I could aesthetically appreciate. So when I'm doing that scene, I can focus on those attractive features and try to block out the rest."

"There has to be something about the person you can find to love," agreed an actor/director/teacher. "The color of their hair, their shoulders, a personality trait." Or you can combine the technique of isolation with the perhaps more difficult technique of substitution. On a nine-month national tour of *The Sound of Music* with a very hateful Ralph, she discovered she had to "think about the person I loved the most in real life and try as close as I could to feel that way about the actor playing Ralph." (Plus, she focused on Ralph's great smile and incredible blue eyes.) For that kind of work, emotional recall stimulated by sense memory is an important tool: certain physical aspects of your co-actor can—if you really work at it—evoke, like Proust's petite madeleine, sensorial impressions of a beloved: his aftershave, her lips, the color of his eyes. Or you can try to mentally cut-and-paste your sweetie's (or, if you don't have a sweetie, Mel Gibson's) features over the features of your co-actor.

One way or another, you have to make isolation or substitution work, advised Los Angeles teacher Judith Weston. "You have to find something to like about him," she said. "Even if all you can come up with is that he's another child of God. That's the actor's job. If the actor doesn't feel inclined to do that, maybe she shouldn't be an actor. You have to be able to look into the other person's eyes and see something human and beautiful."

"Any time you create a relationship," she continued, "you have to use all your resources—your substitutions, your images, your imagination." She referred to Stanislavski's magic "as if": "Ask yourself, what would he have to do to make it up to me so I can forgive him and love him? Imagine [act as if] that has taken place. Maybe in his heart that's how he feels but he can't express it. That's a way to use your imagination to connect." If all else fails, she recommended using the "as if" to close your eyes and pretend Mr. Uncongeniality is your own personal Prince Charming. "Or just look at him and let everything he's doing be new, let all of your history go. That's also an 'as if'— it's as if you're meeting this person for the first time."

Los Angeles teacher Ivana Chubbuck recommends finding ways to identify with your co-actors by sharing personal traumas. This can be done even without your partner's participation, entirely through your own imagination. For details of Chubbuck's unique approach, see Chapter 3, "Chemical Reactions."

Ultimately, your ability to prevent contrary personal feelings from creeping into your art in destructive ways may have a lot to do with maturity.

Said one director, "I think the best definition of professionalism among actors is when they realize they are projecting, that the anger they're feeling toward another actor is something in themselves. This is not a business for immature people, yet immature people tend to go into it." She advised actors to use those bad feelings as an opportunity to see if they're projecting some of their own "past stuff" on others.

Maura Vincent believes there is a reason for an actor finding him- or herself in a hostile situation, and in fact she doesn't allow excuses like "I don't like him" or "It's not working" in her classes. That's life, she says. The truth is that "the more specific and the clearer you are with your own work, the less time and energy you have for not liking or not getting along with the other person." In her class she had a male Asian student who didn't want to work with Asian females. He felt that he was trying to get away from his culture and that Asian students have a reticence approaching acting. "That was difficult for me being Caucasian to deal with," said Vincent. "I told him it was his problem. I stress to my students that when you start to get in trouble, unless it's verging on harassment there's very little you can do about it." Instead, she tells them that there's a window of opportunity for them to learn something. "You need to focus on your own work. The more specific and clearer you are with your work, the less time and energy you have for not liking or not getting along with the other person."

She advises that if you're in a situation with a colleague who is truly causing problems, take all the responsibility onto yourself: "It would be great if you could help me . . ." Do that before you go to the director or to an open forum. If you're in a rehearsal period, refocus for a few days on your own work.

One actor found herself in a two-character play with someone who "came in with an attitude of superiority toward both me and the director." She found it difficult to connect with him because he treated her like a child. "Fortunately there was a great deal of animosity written into the play," she said, "so that fed my character. But after several rehearsals of having everything I said contradicted, my opinions disparaged, I addressed all comments to the director in the form of questions. Which is kind of a chicken-shit way of doing it. But it put the onus of decision making on someone else, and I didn't have to talk to the other actor. Fortunately the director was a master of tact."

What of our students, Tallulah and Marlon, and their befuddled teacher, Constantin? Tallulah was paying for the class and certainly had the right to demand a tension-free learning situation. Unfortunately, she probably would have learned a lot more if she'd stuck with the unsettling Marlon. Both of them could have used the opportunity to sharpen their acting skills and discover more about themselves as artists and individuals.

Chapter 32

STAGE PREPARATION RITUALS

Every actor has his or her own little quirks and rituals, even superstitions, to prepare for a stage performance, and there is no one best method. Some vocalize, some meditate. Yoga devotees may stand on their heads. Others drink herbal tea, with the goal of being relaxed, focused, and energized. Still others, needing to marshal their energy, run in place. One student actor I knew was rumored to routinely masturbate to unwind before his entrance in a Chekhov play. Oy. Of course, the role you're playing, and the given circumstances with which you make your initial entrance, will affect your choice of warm-ups.

Uta Hagen, in *A Challenge for the Actor,* says that our tendency is to bring backstage all the interesting little tidbits of our day. It's true: just as when we were children and brought the details of our day at school to the dinner table, we all want to feel part of our backstage family. But Hagen warns that to join in green room merriment is counterproductive. She arrives at the theatre at least an hour before her call and tries to limit her conversation with colleagues to the play itself. She suggests emptying your mind of the outside world and filling it with your character's life as you apply makeup and get dressed. (Don't think of yourself as putting on a costume, think of yourself as getting dressed in "your" clothing, she advises.)

If you are in a small, crowded backstage area with communal dressing rooms, you may need to get resourceful, even ask the stage manager for help in carving out time or space for yourself. In the theatre where I worked for a long time, actors needing personal warm-up time shut themselves up in the pitch-black backstage furnace room. I knew an actor who always arrived at the theatre fully dressed and made up, didn't say a word to anybody, and wandered the grimy alleys of downtown San Francisco near the theatre until her call. She was considered odd, but who cares? Her performance was great.

Marco Barricelli, in preparing to play the title role in *Hamlet* at the Oregon Shakespeare Festival in Ashland, arrived at the theatre at 5:30 or 6, did stretches "to get my body and blood going," worked slowly on voice and articulators, "but not too much on voice," he said. "If you do too long on vocal warm-up, you'll end up getting your voice more tired." Then he had a fight call, took a shower, and got dressed. He also ate a potato during the long period of time he was offstage, an energy-sustaining habit he borrowed from another Hamlet.

My acting teacher used to have us do jumping jacks to get our energy up before a scene, but I think in actual performance most of us are more interested in chilling out, not getting *more* hyper. Lee Strasberg used to teach whole classes that consisted of nothing but relaxation and breathing exercises.

Barnard Hughes said in an interview in *Actors on Acting* that he likes to just sit and be quiet and think about the play at the point at which he entered. He said that E.G. Marshall did yoga, but that he himself prayed, not only for help, but to offer up his work to God. He also noted in the old days, stage actors had nothing to do all day but rest, eat, and sleep, whereas nowadays actors are busy with auditions, commercial shoots, etc., which makes it harder to summon the right energy.

One nervous actor said she steadies herself by leaning into a wall, feet away from the wall, pressing her hands against it and breathing. Her last stop: the bathroom. (But I've heard of actors who prefer to go onstage with a full bladder; it gives them that extra obstacle, I guess. Whatever works.)

Another actor does a set of tai chi stretches for fifteen minutes, and simultaneously does a voice warm-up with yawning, diaphragmatic breathing, articulation drill, and tongue twisters. After costume and makeup, he takes fifteen minutes to walk "in the character," recalling key concerns and responding sotto voce to the actual world around him backstage. "Then in the ten minutes just before I go on," he said, "I do a set of primary emotion gestures, empty my mind, and begin acting the first intention."

Yet another confided, "I pace vigorously, going over the first two lines of my part a billion times, throw up, pee, and do the whole thing once again." Different strokes, eh?

An actor obliged to share a small theatre's dressing room with mostly men for *Ballad of a Sad Cafe* struggled to feel private, "the aloneness of a woman among the crowd."

Some people nosh before a show—I once shared a dressing room with a beautiful young woman who ate nothing but chocolate bars on performance days, right up to curtain time—and others are ready to barf at the sight of food. But I and many others drank coffee. One actor's doctor-father advised him to eat a banana before every show. Something about the potassium . . .

An actor told me she does either vocal and facial exercises while driving to or while at the theatre, runs her lines fast while dressing, and, if the role is dramatic, spends a little time alone doing deep breathing just before going on stage.

Everyone I talked to seems to have latched onto a nightly ritual that apparently varies only according to the show, not necessarily according to how they feel *that night.* Yet in his book *An Acrobat of the Heart (A Physical Approach to Acting Inspired by the Work of Jerzy Grotowski)*, New York University acting teacher Stephen Wangh commented, "A warm-up is a bridge between the conditions of mind, body, and voice you need in order to act. The nature of that bridge depends on who you are and what your particular voice, body, and psyche need today, so no two actors are likely to need exactly the same type of warm-up. Moreover, the kind of bridge you need on a particular day also depends on where you are 'coming from' . . ." The context of his remarks is a discussion of rehearsal techniques, but I think they can just as easily apply to pre-show warm-ups. He goes on to say, "and the week you are rehearsing Pinter, your warm-up will probably need to be different from the one you require before commedia dell'arte rehearsals." He says that a warm-up is a fluid process; you need to try different things to find out what works for you in different circumstances.

Any warm-up no-no's? I knew a woman who, to get it up for a flirtatious role, invaded the men's dressing room and routinely goosed her male colleagues who were trying to prepare. There's a point where one actor's preparation can adversely infringe upon another's.

Wangh also offers a caveat: Make sure you're not doing relaxation exercises as a way to avoid getting in touch with your sources of energy. Both relaxation and energy are required for good acting.

Chapter 33

CRITICAL THINKING: THEIRS

It happens all the time: Two critics see the exact same opening-night performance. One says you were brilliant; the other says you sucked. What gives? I called up a few reviewers to find out the answer to this and other mysteries that actors obsess about.

The critics I talked to agreed on several things:

1. It's hard to figure out whether the director or the actor him/herself is responsible for a particular aspect of a given performance. "Something you don't like . . . may have been foisted on the actor by the director, or maybe there was very little rehearsal time, but it's difficult to get away from assigning credit or blame," said *Variety* theatre critic Dennis Harvey. Agreed another, "It's hard to tell if it's an acting thing or if they've been directed that way. Sometimes I feel like I can suss that out; other times it's more difficult."

2. It's nearly impossible to articulate a set of actual guidelines for judging actors. "I sit there thinking that I know good craftsmanship from bad the minute I see it, that there are some kind of objective standards, yet it's clear there aren't," said the *San Francisco Chronicle*'s Robert Hurwitt. "It always surprises me to see a performance that is unfocused, or terribly mannered, or not thought through, that other critics will rave about."

3. It's as puzzling to critics as it is to actors why two reviewers can see the same performance from opposing viewpoints. Hurwitt, a former actor, said he was once reviewed by two critics on the same night; one said he spoke too quickly, the other said he was the only one in the cast with the proper diction. "I think all actors should read their reviews in that light," Hurwitt laughed.

4. Theoretically, what a critic had for lunch should not affect how he or she feels about a show. But *L.A. Weekly* senior theatre editor Steven Leigh Morris related this story: "A colleague had a migraine for a week. Then he got medication for it, went to review a play, adored it, and wrote a rave. Everyone else panned it, and he felt quite embarrassed. He realized he'd been reviewing his medication, not the play. If someone has the flu going in, they're not going to have a good time, and it's rotten when the actor gets blamed. Some critics can see past that, but we're human."

Not only are critics actually human, many have credentials that prove they understand theatre from an insider's perspective. Morris himself has an MFA in playwriting from UCLA. Hurwitt performed with the San Francisco Mime Troupe for two years during its early days, cofounded a street theatre company in London, and appeared in a few plays in Berkeley in the late '70s. "With a play I've read or seen before or performed in, obviously I have certain ideas about the characters," Hurwitt said. "When I see actors perform a part I know well and they make me feel I'm seeing it for the first time, I'm humbled. [But if] I feel there's so much this actor is *not* getting out of the role, that's the basis for my criticizing the performance."

Like Hurwitt, Kerry Reid, a Chicago critic, has an acting background (eight years with small companies in Chicago). "I see actors do parts they're not quite right for. I assume they've taken the part because they're trying to stretch, and I'll be more forgiving," Reid said. "If you want a long career, you've got to learn to take those risks. I know how hard it is to get work."

All copped to certain preferences and prejudices, from the general (Harvey prefers to see older performers playing down in age rather than younger actors playing older characters, because "the older performers have much more training and can more easily move into other role ages without a lot of superficial affectations") to the specific (Morris loved Max Wright's "bucketful of eccentricities" in the Los Angeles production of *The Cripple of Inishmaan* but was annoyed by Ian McKellen's "load of mannerisms" in *Enemy of the People* at the Ahmanson, although the *L.A. Times* praised Sir Ian).

Most agreed that it's important that all the actors in a given play be acting in a similar style, one that's appropriate for the material, and that it's the director's responsibility to make sure they are. "The sort of things that would be annoying in a realistic Lanford Wilson play, like mugging, would be perfect in a Charles Busch play," commented Morris, "and it's really annoying when a truthful actor uses that realistic style in a broad comedy." Added Hurwitt, "A discrepancy in styles of acting . . . frequently happens in companies that have not been integrated over the years."

Harvey likes it when actors know how to "be in the background"—that is, participate in a scene when the attention is on others without appearing awkward.

"I look for how actors relate to each other onstage," commented Hurwitt. He cites danger signals: "An actor who doesn't know what to do with her hands . . . actors who lose focus when they're not speaking . . . problems with acting drunk . . . actors whose bodies and voices seem unaffected by the climate and time of day if it's a realistic play . . . actors who haven't learned how to use their vocal or physical instrument."

Reid expanded on that to include a failure to scale performances, vocally and physically, to the venue. "I notice this more with comic performances. I don't like to be bludgeoned into laughing," she said.

She commented, too, on appropriate style: "I look for comfort with language in the classics. Does it seem natural in their mouths? Sometimes I see actors take a little pause before they say a line that's out-of-date slang; it gives the effect of commenting on it."

I should add here that I myself write capsule reviews for *Back Stage West.* Having been trained in a realistic, Method-based technique, I look for believability above all—and I don't care whether you're using Anne Bogart's Viewpoints, or Tadashi Suzuki's techniques, or a Jacques Lecoq approach, or whatever. When an actor is convincing—whether in a kitchen-sink drama, a Greek tragedy, Brecht, or theatre of the absurd—the audience just knows it. As Steven Leigh Morris explained, "We're looking for a kind of truth, but that doesn't mean naturalism, that's not a comment about style. What makes actors credible is the ability to persuade us—if their energy is coming from a place that's true."

Are reviewers influenced by being told the specific circumstances of a production? Reid said she's more forgiving if she knows there have been cast changes or technical problems and thinks most reviewers are more forgiving than not. "There's so much we're not privy to," she sighed.

All the critics I talked to understood that it's hard not to take reviews personally, but they sort of wish you wouldn't anyway. "It should always be kept in mind that no one's opinion counts for more than a single vote," said Dennis Harvey. "Any critic who thinks his or her opinion is definitive is sadly misinformed."

Observed Hurwitt, "In the same way an actor is seeking some kind of truth in a role, we're seeking some kind of truth in our writing. I think our reviews should be read in that spirit rather than as judgments."

Well said—although easier said than done, eh?

Chapter 34

CRITICAL THINKING: YOURS

A review in the *San Francisco Chronicle* of the musical *Pippin* was devastating. At the end, the critic mentioned that the same (new-in-town) producing team would be staging two more musicals this season. He concluded with, "Be afraid. Be very afraid."

Ouch. The production did sound really cheesy, but I couldn't help feeling sorry for the hapless producers, who put their heart and soul—not to mention tons of money—into the show.

As actors, we don't put money into the show—quite the reverse, hopefully—but in most cases we do put our heart and soul into it. And if we've been in the business for a while, we've probably gotten our share of bad reviews. But as stage performers, we have to go back on stage the very next night, often (compared to musicians and dancers) for a long run. Talk about nerves of steel!

"You never forget the bad reviews," sighed Don Took, a longtime actor with South Coast Repertory. Upon request, he intoned, "'Don Took was unexceptional as an unexceptional father,'" citing a *Los Angeles Times* review for Nicky Silver's *Pterodactyls.* "Some people said that's not a bad review, and I thought bullshit," he said. In a review of another play, that same critic called him "excellent."

An actor I know expects her epitaph to be "Woefully miscast"—from a bad review she got twenty-five years ago and still remembers verbatim. Another actor I know obsessed endlessly over an enigmatic review that said he went "in and out like a shaky radio signal."

A third, Michael Sullivan, told me he was criticized for having "bulging neck veins"—"like it's something you can control on stage!" He also said, "When I did my one-person show, I knew I'd overwritten one section and was overcompensating by overacting. All the critics gave me excellent reviews but picked that part that bugged them. I was disappointed that everyone noticed it, but it didn't bother me; it was like, yeah, I know. It depends on how big your ego is and how you can take those kinds of blows. Harder for me is when I'm left out of reviews—especially when I'm the lead!" In one show that got good reviews, the main daily said something like, "Oh, and Michael Sullivan is in the show."

A good rule of thumb is that if you are the type to stew, don't read the reviews until after the show, if at all. Susannah Schulman made a pact with a fellow actor to ignore the reviews of a particular show she was in. "But we found that pretending that reviews don't exist is an impossible task," she admitted. "Curiosity overtakes you like an insidious disease. We had a complete breakdown of integrity and read absolutely every review." Luckily, they were good.

In what ways can reviews have a negative effect? Well, if it's a bad review, it can undermine your confidence and influence you to change your performance. Plenty of actors do so. But Schulman, for one, thinks this is a bad idea under any circumstances.

"But what if you think the critic has a point?" I argued.

"It's kind of too bad," said Schulman. "You signed on to complete the director's vision in conjunction with your own vision. There's trust involved. Changing things wouldn't be fair to anyone else in the production."

"But what if your trust in the director isn't there?"

"Even if you're feeling unsure, by opening night you've come to a certain place with it," she replied. "Otherwise you've got five more weeks of sheer torture."

"Well, what if the criticism isn't anything that would affect anyone but you? For example, maybe the critic said you're talking too loud."

"If I tried to change my performance, every time I opened my mouth, I'd be thinking, is it now he thought I was talking too loud? Or now?" replied Schulman. "Would he think I'm talking too softly now? It's giving them too much power," she concluded.

Conversely, a good review can be disruptive. Amy Hill got great reviews for her solo show *Tokyo Bound*. (Normally she doesn't read reviews during the run, but in this case she had to because she was also producing.) "I had the stress of knowing people were reading this and expecting the show to be brilliant," she said. "I wondered if I could live up to the reviews." Agreed Geoff Elliott, of Los Angeles' A Noise Within, "You become self-conscious about a particular moment. Or you go on thinking you're god's gift to the acting world, and then you trip over yourself."

Equally unsettling is receiving both good and bad reviews simultaneously. One critic praised Amy Hill in her first singing role in *Follies*, while another critic trashed her. "I think I was in between brilliant and horrible," she laughed. "For things like that, you have to trust your director." She thinks reviews, whether good or bad, take the focus off the work. "[Someone told me] just before I went on, 'Did you read the review in the *Los Angeles Times*? They hated the show.' I'm thinking, What is your focus on? We have to go onstage and be in those moments together, and that's all that exists for us. I just wanted to kill him. It was inappropriate to talk to me about it." In fact, she usually announces to the cast in advance, "If you want to talk about the reviews, please do it outside."

There's also the embarrassment of being the only one in the cast to get a good review in a show that's been panned. Schulman described that situation as "truly annoying. . . . When everyone is talking about the review—and this is admitting a human weakness, a vulnerability on my part—you want to say, 'Well, it wasn't *all* bad.'" Which, of course, would turn your green room friends into enemies.

At A Noise Within, co-artistic directors Art Manke, Geoff Elliott, and Julia Rodriguez-Elliott discovered that the cast tended to become obsessed by reviews. "They spent all their time rationalizing why they got a good review or why they got dumped on," explained Elliott. "We aren't able to keep our eye on the ball because we become obsessed." So a theatre policy was established to neither post nor discuss the reviews within the building. "Inside the building our job is to create art. It may not work for some, but [outlawing discussion of reviews] works for us."

At South Coast Rep, everybody reads the reviews but there's an unspoken agreement not to discuss them on the job.

On the side of taking the reviews seriously if not to heart, longtime actor Dean Goodman, who does read reviews, suggested examining the review to see if there's any truth in it, and work on that. "Sometimes there isn't much you can do," he said. "Maybe discuss it with your director. If you're certain it isn't true or that there isn't much you can do, just follow your instincts." He remembered a review that was entirely about him, about how badly he'd overacted. "Many members of the cast thought I'd be too shattered to go on. But I did. But at that same time another review came out which said I played the role with consummate artistry." Who you're going to believe probably goes to your ego strength.

I asked Don Took, who's gotten very few bad reviews in a long career, if consistently bad reviews could make an actor quit the business. "I've never known an actor to quit for that reason," he said, "although people might stop casting you." I also asked him if bad reviews hurt less as you get older. "If your passion and emotion are involved, if you're totally on board, you're going to hurt if the show gets a bad review," he told me. "That's the nature of being a team player and being part of a project that you're invested in." Schulman too mentioned her emotional involvement in what kind of reviews the entire production receives. And another actor told me she suffered most from a bad review not for herself but for a show she deeply believed in, and which was well received by audiences.

But some experienced actors have gotten to a place where the reviews don't bother them. Half-joked one, who'd recently received lavish praise for his role in Harold Pinter's *The Homecoming*, "When the reviews are really bad, I believe them, and when they're really good, I think I fooled 'em again!" But he added that in general he's very cold-blooded about reviews, and advises that if they're important to you, you probably shouldn't read them. Schulman added, "It used to be that the goods were too good to me and the bads were too bad. Now I've come to a place where I can think, Oh, it's great they think that, or, Oh, that's too bad, but I don't think it'll affect ticket sales."

"I suppose the original cast of *Oedipus* probably worried about [reviews]," mused Elliott. "I heard Michael Feingold of the *Village Voice* speaking once. He said, 'Let it go, my voice is one voice, it's my opinion.' Understand and embrace that! The greatest actors living and passed on have all been dumped on, so you're in good company. Our job is about pursuing a passion-filled objective. Ultimately we're storytellers. A part of that is about getting outside yourself, pursuing an objective."

How to get to that cool mind-set? Therapist and former actor Armand Volkas conceded, "I think keeping one's equilibrium in this business in the sense of self-esteem based on your own values is a real challenge. . . . I think one needs to develop a screening mechanism where you either don't read the reviews, or you know what triggers you. If you tend to obsess, have somebody you trust read the review and tell you if it's something you want to hear, or have them just read you the good parts." He pointed out that this is not the final statement about you: "It's about putting it in perspective."

That might work for some people, although I tend to agree with the actor who said, "Sometimes I wonder about people who insist they don't read the reviews—I have a hard time believing them. I couldn't take it if people were comforting me about something I haven't even read." Interestingly, she compared bad reviews to tough audiences: Every audience is different, some more responsive than others. "Sometimes actors will complain about an audience," she said, "and you can see them bending their performance out of shape, contorting it" to try and please. "If the audience is not really responding in the way I've become accustomed to based on other audiences, I say to myself, Just do the show. I'm not going to mug, or go really fast, running through beats so I can get offstage. I just remind myself of the basics: Listen to what the other person is saying, and be as clear as I can in responding to them, and leave it at that."

Finally, Chris Wells of Los Angeles' Actors' Gang—which does post reviews—told me of a mortifying slam he once received for playing Orson Welles in *Euphoria*. "I got a call from a friend who'd seen the review and told me not to read it. I, unlike other actors, read all reviews. I can't stand that people know information that I don't. I went to Mayfair Market, looked at the stack, said to myself, Am I really prepared? Picked it up, opened it, read the review: 'Wells' slimy portrayal . . . is about as amusing as animal droppings on a living room rug.' It was so ridiculously heavy handed and mean spirited that by the time I got to the animal droppings part I was howling in the Mayfair Market. I thought there was something going on more than his response to the play." Wells' reaction was entirely healthy: "Instead of just sitting with it, I read it to people. I eventually had it blown up and framed. It is my dream to one day hang it above my toilet!" He advised, "Think of reviews as publicity. They're totally separate from the work." He added ruefully, "I wish I was a strong enough person to not read them."

And the hapless producers of *Pippin*? They were never heard from again in San Francisco.

Chapter 35

THE UNBEARABLE NEUROSIS OF ACTING

"I don't like what [acting] brings to the surface in my personality: the self-centeredness, the childish vanity, the infantilism. That's what an actor has to have." So said the late, influential acting teacher Sandy Meisner (quoted in *Sanford Meisner on Acting*).

I can relate.

I gave up acting (and acting, for me, was like a dream come true) partly because, like Meisner, I felt it was consistently activating negative personality traits. As time went by, I found I didn't want just good reviews, I wanted four-star raves. I didn't want to be told I was good, I wanted to be told I was a Jewish Meryl Streep. For every part I didn't get, even if I didn't want it, I could've used a megadose of Prozac. In short, I was insatiable.

But is Meisner right in saying it has to be this way?

Psychotherapist and drama therapist (and former actor) Armand Volkas wasn't surprised when I quoted Meisner to him. He compared actors to children who adapt their personality to please their parents and thus develop a false self. "That's an oversimplified explanation," he said, "but I do think a lot of actors go into the business to try to get unconscious needs met. That's where it becomes dysfunctional. When you put up with rejection and humiliation, and when approval is based on the whims of a casting director or a director, and you aren't centered or grounded in your real self, that's when you lose your equilibrium."

My acting teacher, Jean Shelton, once told us that after some soul searching, she realized that the reason she'd become an actor in the first place was to win her father's approval. She advised us all to think about why we wanted to act. If you believe that self-knowledge—discovering your unconscious needs—is power, Shelton's advice makes sense.

"Acting is a very self-absorbing career," conceded Los Angeles actor-turned-playwright Laurel Ollstein. "I never noticed it so much until I began to write and watch actors go through the process in my plays. It's incredible to listen to actors after a reading. They truly see the play only from their own character's point of view." She believes that this is not only necessary for the actor, it's also useful to the writer. But she noticed that when she went back to acting, those same self-centered feelings materialized. Actors are, at least temporarily, children—so if they happen to have a spouse and actual child, it can be difficult. Ollstein once appeared in a play with her daughter and found it hard to split her focus, "being Mom and wanting to be the actor." She said she doesn't find that split with writing.

Amy Hill, who creates funny and honest solo shows based on her personal experiences, sees what Meisner called "infantilism" in a positive light. To her, it can mean open, curious, listening, in touch with your feelings. "The benefit of age is being able to channel those qualities," she said. "As a child, it comes out in whatever way it does: screaming, peeing on the carpet. I feel as though the older I get and the more comfortable I am in my own skin, the better actor I've become. Not that I'm self-centered, but I've given myself permission to be more self-aware."

Hill said her only problem is that in a weird way, she doesn't like a lot of attention. "I'm uncomfortable with a lot of people talking to me that I don't know," she explained. "I enjoy the process of acting and the energy between actor and audience. So when people come up after the show and talk to me, it stresses me out—and then I eat. I think the better I feel about me, the better I am offstage—and onstage too. The two personae have blended a little bit more as I mature."

Added Hill, who is half Japanese, "One of the banes of existence for an actor of color is the perception that we're all extras. When I tell people on the street that I'm an actor, they say, 'Oh? Do you have lines?' We go to the set and they say, 'The extras parking is over there,' and I'm like, 'I'm in the cast! I'm one of the stars!' And you wonder, is this an ego thing coming up? You start getting more sensitive about all kinds of weird stuff."

She also observed, "I think many actors, despite the common perception, go into acting not for the fame but because it fulfills their creative need to express themselves. And then when people start telling you you're brilliant, you start judging yourself based on what other people say. You have to not base your sense of worth on that, or on whether you're currently working, or doing a good or a stupid project, stage or film, or whatever." Hill recommends psychotherapy if you're feeling at the mercy of emotional ups and downs, a survival mechanism that has worked well for her. The other key is to have an outside life. "The people I know whose lives are entirely involved with acting and theatre are crazy," she said.

"I think we all get testy with the pressure," acknowledged another actor. "You're being scrutinized. Who else gets reviewed on their job every time? And you're always going back to square one. You get great reviews in one show, but you're back to auditioning. . . . You think, Why do I put myself through this?"

Paige Pengra, who worked in film, TV, and theatre in Los Angeles for ten years, was on the brink of being one of those "crazy" actors. "The business of acting really exacerbated all of my fears and insecurities," she said. "I resented that I was at the beck and call of whoever wanted to see me. I felt powerless. I was also extraordinarily body-conscious. . . . I was watching everybody's neurosis come out. It was sad and hilarious. I saw how people deal with authority, I watched people become other people's mothers and fathers . . . the egomaniacal, narcissistic directors who are willing to abuse whoever to get what they want onstage . . . It can be a terrible experience."

In college, acting had been a great source of joy for her, even a spiritual experience. But in Los Angeles, when she and a group of women colleagues met for weekly lunches, they griped about their latest awful audition, how short the director wanted their skirts to be, how much money they were pouring into their careers. "We didn't have anybody who could facilitate a process where we could empower ourselves," she said.

But during a long run at the Matrix Theatre, she had an eye-opening positive experience: "I was coming out of a bad relationship and I was playing a character who was jilted, set up, and framed. I was able to go almost melodramatic Greek tragedy in this farce, and it was a faster healing process for me."

Intrigued by a vision of theatre's therapeutic potential, she headed to Dell'Arte's drama therapy workshop in Northern California. When I talked to her, she was finishing a master's degree in therapy in San Francisco (her thesis was called "Person and persona negotiating balance in a professional actor's life through the use of drama therapy") and planning to return to Los Angeles to create support groups for actors who are "lost in the turbulent lifestyle." She said, "I don't think I'll go back to acting the way that it was."

Me neither. For what it's worth, and at the risk of appearing, well, self-centered by using myself as an example, I'll add that I feel less like a needy child when I'm writing than I ever did when I was acting. That, of course, is partly because I am no longer artistically repressed: Unlike artists, writers, singers, and musicians, actors (and also filmmakers and directors) cannot practice their chosen craft unless someone allows them to do so. (The exception, of course, is those who raise the money to self-produce, which necessitates wearing an additional, producer's hat.)

Such is the plight of the actor. So, have we decided whether actors are inevitably self-centered and infantile, as Meisner apparently believed, or whether such traits only manifest themselves in some unstable types who maybe need a good shrink?

Neither nor, says Eric Maisel, a therapist and author specializing in issues of creativity. He believes there are two types of narcissism—healthy and unhealthy. "All creative people are mixed narcissists," he said firmly. "We have a nice chunk of healthy narcissism and an unfortunate chunk of unhealthy narcissism. Part of the reason the subject is confusing is because people talk about it without the adjectives, as if it's just pejorative. But narcissism is something a child and adult *ought* to have.

"The task for an actor," he continued, "is to minimize the unhealthy without eroding the healthy. It's a task because when we try to become more generous, more compassionate, more this or that, we can also lose ourselves and not be as self-directing and independent and strong as we need to be."

That's why no actor is going to become a completely healthy narcissist. The goal is to achieve a manageable ratio of healthy to unhealthy narcissism. "So rather than looking at a movement from self-centered actor to egoless actor," explained Maisel, "the movement is from the self-centered actor to the more balanced but still narcissistic actor."

To begin to achieve this modicum of balance, the first thing is to be aware of the problem, advised Maisel. "It's not that hard to make intuitive distinctions between when you're being strong and independent and when you're being a jerk," he said. "You've got to notice it and decide to uphold the one thing and minimize the other thing."

Meanwhile: Time for graham crackers and milk, everybody.

BIBLIOGRAPHY

Adler, Stella, et al. 2000. *The Art of Acting.* New York: Applause Theatre Book Publishers.

Brine, Adrian. 2000. *A Shakespearean Actor Prepares.* Lyme, NH: Smith & Kraus.

Carlson, Steve. 1998. *Hitting Your Mark.* Studio City, CA: Michael Wiese Productions.

Carnovsky, Morris. 1984. *The Actor's Eye.* New York: Performing Arts Journal Publications.

Chekhov, Michael. 1991. *On the Technique of Acting.* New York: HarperCollins.

Cohen, Robert. 1978. *Acting Power.* New York: McGraw-Hill.

Hagen, Uta. 1973. *Respect for Acting.* New York: Macmillan.

Hagen, Uta. 1991. *A Challenge for the Actor.* New York: Scribner.

Kalter, Joanmarie. 1980. *Actors on Acting.* New York: Sterling Publishing Co.

Maisel, Eric. 2002. *Van Gogh Blues.* Emmaus, PA: Rodale Press.

Meisner, Sanford, with Dennis Longwell. 1987. *Sanford Meisner on Acting.* New York: Vintage Books.

Moore, Sonia. 1962. *The Stanislavski Method.* New York: Viking Books.

Wangh, Stephen. 2000. *An Acrobat of the Heart (A Physical Approach to Acting Inspired by the Work of Jerzy Grotowski).* New York: Vintage Books.

Weston, Judith. 1996. *Directing Actors.* Studio City, CA: Michael Wiese Productions.